FLY FISHING
the lifetime sport

By

David and Cheryl Young

Young, David W.
Young, Cheryl

Fly Fishing: the Lifetime Sport/David W. and Cheryl Young

Includes glossary, bibliography references and index

Special thanks to Sage, Bucks Bags, and EMR Drift Boats for making such
fine products, and for providing some of their photos.

Also special thanks to Gary DeMille for layout and design.

Table of Contents

TACKLE 1

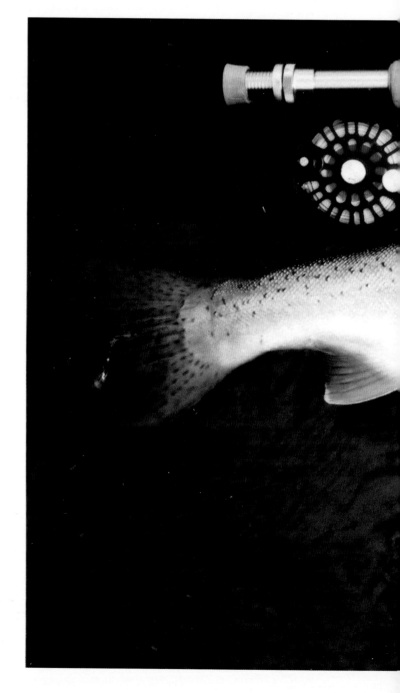

Rods

Because fly fishing manufacturers offer hundreds of different rods for sale, choosing the right rod for you can be perplexing, even frustrating. All fly rods, however, differ primarily in their actions, in the materials of their construction, and in their lengths.

Rod makers classify the basic actions of their rods as slow, medium, and fast. A slow action rod flexes throughout its tip, mid, and butt sections. A medium action rod flexes primarily in its mid and tip sections. A fast action rod flexes primarily in its tip section.

On their rods, all reputable rod makers list the weight of line the rod will cast. The first thirty feet of a fly line weighs a uniform weight, and the rod's action is balanced to cast this known and specified weight. All manufacturers of fly lines designate uniform numbers for the weights of their lines. Regardless of maker, fly lines come in weights from one to fifteen. Consequently, all fly rods, fly lines, and fly reels are matched to these weight designations: the smaller the number, the lighter the line weight. Below, I've listed common line and rod weights according to their uses:

1-2 Weight Lines and Rods

Designed for casting to small fish at short distances. In addition, these rods are designed to make delicate deliveries for tiny flies. Best for small trout and panfish like bluegills and crappies.

3 Weight Lines and Rods

Designed for casting short to medium distances with small flies; used for trout and panfish.

4 Weight Lines and Rods

Designed for casting medium sized flies delicately at medium distances; used for trout and panfish.

5 Weight Lines and Rods

Designed for accurately casting short, medium, and long distances with a wide size range of flies. Effective for trout, panfish, smallmouth bass, largemouth bass.

6 Weight Lines and Rods

A general all-around rod with many uses; designed for casting all distances well. Can be used for trout, pan-fish, bass, and steelhead.

7-8 Weight Lines and Rods

Designed for casting long distances for very large trout, bass, and big fish up to about fifteen pounds, including Atlantic and Pacific salmon and steelhead.

9-10 Weight Lines and Rods

Designed for casting long distances with large flies for heavy fish of thirty to forty pounds: bonefish, permit, striped bass, bonito, albacore, bluefish, redfish, and snook.

11-15 Weight Lines and Rods

Heavy salt water rods for large fish: billfish, tarpon, etc..

Rod makers manufacture rods using a variety of materials: fiberglass, bamboo, graphite, and graphite composites (which may include boron or titanium). Graphite rods are the most popular because of their light weights and relatively inexpensive costs and the wide assortment of weights and sizes.

Fiberglass rods are rarely used because of their limited choices of actions and heavier weights. Bamboo rods are costly because of their complex manufacturing process. In addition, bamboo rods weigh more than graphite and fiberglass rods and their actions tend to be slower than the graphite's. The boron and titanium graphite composites are unusually strong fly rods with quick recovery rates. These rods cast well both short and long distances.

Rod lengths can vary from six to fifteen feet in length. A short rod (under eight feet) is well suited to fish the small, brushy streams with overhanging vegetation. A medium length fly rod (eight to nine feet), however, is the most versatile and can be used to fish both small and large streams. The longer rods (9 1/2-15 feet) are specialized rods used to make high backcasts required under some conditions. These long rods nevertheless make handling line much easier than shorter rods do.

Windy areas call for high line speeds to cut through the wind. Fast action rods more easily create fast line speeds than medium and slow action rods, although good casters can create high line speeds with even the slowest action rods.

A beginning caster will almost always

cast farther with a fast action rod whereas an accomplished caster can make long casts with slow, medium, or fast action rods. On the other hand, slower action rods create delicate fly presentations more easily than fast action rods.

Regardless, big fish and big flies are easier to control with faster action rods. Truly large fish can require longer and faster action rods to lift and move them.

In addition, fast action rods generate tighter loops than slower actions, and in casting, loop size is important. The tighter or narrower the loop, the more efficiently the line sails through the air. Wide loops create more air resistance simply because of their larger surface area. Tight loops cast farther with faster line speeds than wider loops, although delicacy of presentation suffers from high line speeds.

Slower action rods cushion the stress on light tippets. Faster action rods need heavier, stronger tippets.

Because fast action rods demand precise timing in the casting stroke, a medium action rod is the best choice for a beginner. For one thing, a medium action rod is more forgiving than a fast action rod, and with a medium action rod, a beginning caster can still make a good cast even if his or her timing is a little off.

When purchasing a rod, take into account where you will be using it. How windy is the environment on an average day? How well do you cast? How large are the fish you intend to catch and the flies you intend to use?

The fly fishing manufacturers have perfected their trade, and nearly every rod sold today is of good quality. All of the name brand manufacturers sell quality rods in both their entry-level rods and in their high end products. Simply put, choose a rod in your price range and buy from a name brand manufacturer. Select a rod action and a rod length appropriate to your fishing conditions.

Reels

Manufacturers also have an abundance of quality reels on the market. The basic reel types feature regular arbor spools or wide arbor spools with either a pawl drag or disc drag system.

The spool circumference of a regular arbor reel decreases rapidly as a fish takes out the line. This loss of line and decrease in the reel's circumference creates a corresponding increase in drag pressure. Loss of line and loss of circumference translate into a loss of leverage. In other words, as the spool's diameter shrinks, the drag tension increases. In addition, the weight of the extended line in the water increases the force and pull on a fighting fish. These forces can be an advantage because they naturally and smoothly increase the drag tension on a fighting fish. You don't have to fiddle with the reel's drag adjustment, although this increase in drag may break a light tippet. If you're using a heavy tippet, however, this tension increase aids in slowing down an active fish. Nevertheless, the smaller circumferences of regular sized arbor reels make them slow at retrieving line. Slow retrieval speed can create a slack line and become downright cumbersome if a fish swims rapidly towards you.

Wide arbor reels lessen this natural increase in tension because their spool circumferences are bigger. This size increase in circumference results in a decrease in drag tension as the fish takes out line, always an advantage when fishing light tippets. A

wide arbor reel experiences fewer changes in drag tension as the line and backing leave the spool. The net result is a stable drag tension. Furthermore, the wide arbor reel retrieves line much faster than a regular sized arbor reel. As a fish runs towards you, you can better keep up with it and retrieve the slack line.

Wide arbor reels weigh more than regular arbor reels and the heavier weight can off-set the balance of the rod and reel, making the outfit "reel heavy." This added weight can become annoying after a long day of fishing. A wide arbor reel also has less room to hold backing.

When fishing for larger fish with heavy tippets, I prefer a regular arbor reel although large arbor reels do a better job of protecting light tippets.

A pawl drag system is designed to keep a light tension on the reel spool and to prevent the spool from overrunning and backlashing. Pawl drag systems, however, lack a wide range of heavy drag settings, but they are nevertheless adequate for most freshwater fishing conditions.

Disc drag systems, by contrast, have a wide range of heavy drag adjustments; consequently, they excel when heavy pressure must be applied. Flyfishers use disc drag reels for the larger freshwater and all saltwater fish species. Because disc drag reels must be precisely engineered to maintain a smooth and constant pressure at heavy settings, these reels cost more and weigh more than pawl drag reels.

Lines

All fly lines are sold in weight numbers that correspond to a particular rod's slow, medium, or fast action. Simply match the line weight designation to the rod's action weight number. For example, a five-weight line is designed to cast well with a five-weight rod. The line and rod manufacturers have standardized the number designations. Be careful, however, to avoid confusing a line's weight with a sinking line's sink rate number. They do not match. The sink rate number refers to the rate of speed at which the line sinks; likewise, the line's weight number is based upon the actual weight in grains of the first thirty feet of line.

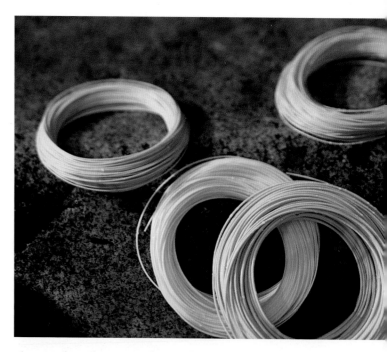

Floating Lines

Floating lines float because they are less dense than water. Their coating contains tiny air bubbles.

Line makers manufacture three basic types of lines: level, double taper, and weight forward.

Level lines are used primarily for shooting or running lines; moreover, level lines are used in conjunction with shooting heads. Because a smaller diameter line has less surface area and less friction as it shoots through the guides, flyfishers generally prefer small diameter level lines. Level lines are inexpensive but seldom used as fly lines. Because they lack any tapers, casts with level lines make poor deliveries.

Double taper lines are seldom used, either. True, this is an oversight because double tapers excel at mending, accuracy, and distance. Double tapers also maintain controlled loops and casting form with ease. Unfortunately, double taper lines are larger in volume and quickly fill up a reel spool, leaving less room for backing than weight forward lines. Most fishermen overlook the double tapers and buy the weight forward lines because they think that the "rocket-taper" will improve their casting. The uniform belly thickness and uniform mass of double tapers, however, transmit the casting loop forces evenly. Double tapered lines also last longer. When one taper wears out, the owner can "reverse" the line on the reel by pulling it all off and tying the most heavily used portion

onto the spool or backing. For distance casting, I use a line one weight smaller than my rod's designation. This allows the rod to control a longer line because the line weights are determined by the actual weight in grains of the first thirty feet of line. A line one weight class smaller than the rod's recommended line is longer, so I might use a four weight line on a five weight rod.

Considering their sales numbers, weight forward lines are the most popular. They have a short double taper section up front with a smaller diameter level running line behind. With the weight of the line up front, a weight forward line is designed to shoot this short double tapered section towards its target. The standard weight forward line has thirty feet in its weight forward section but the remainder of the line is a level shooting line. Other specialized lines have longer weight forward sections up to and over forty feet in length. Because these lines cast more like a double taper up close and because they can cast farther, I prefer these kinds of weight forward lines. Scientific Anglers markets these lines as "distance tapers" and Cortland calls them "long belly lines." Performing nearly as well as a double taper, the distance tapers take up less room on the reel spool and allow the spool to hold more backing.

Sinking Lines

Essential for fishing still waters, sinking lines come in standard sink and uniform sink designations.

A standard sink line's belly section sinks deeper than its thinner ends. When fully sunk, the belly of the line is deeper than the end of the fly line, which causes the fly and leader to buoy up above the line's belly. This buoyancy has its advantages and disadvantages. Suspending the fly up off the bottom makes the fly more visible to the fish and less likely to catch weeds. On the other hand, you may miss strikes because the line's arch makes it difficult to detect the bite of a soft-taking fish or to react to a very quick take.

The uniform sink lines sink evenly with the belly and tip sections at the same depth. A uniform sinking line can place your fly inside the weed beds but the fly may constantly snag. Hidden in weeds, your fly is less visible to the fish. Furthermore, a fly adorned with weeds is rarely taken. The big advantage of a uniform sinking line is the straight line it creates between you and the fish. Generally speaking, you can more easily detect soft strikes from fish with a uniform sinking line than with a standard sinking line.

When fishing heavily weeded areas, I prefer the standard sinking line because my fly catches fewer weeds and more fish, but when fishing over a clean bottom, I prefer a uniform sinking line because it detects more strikes.

Sinking lines also come in weight forward and shooting head styles. (I'm unaware of any double tapers.) Shooting heads are usually thirty feet in length, and they are joined to running line or to monofilament.

Manufacturers issue sinking lines with a variety of sinking rates. Sinking lines are numbered as intermediate, 1, 2, 3, 4, 5, and 6. In addition, deep water express and lead core lines are also available. The following table lists sink rates and suspension depths:

The line choice controls your fly's sinking rate and suspension depth. To sink your fly

Line	Sink Rate (inches per second)	Suspension Depth (feet)
Intermediate	less 1 inch	0-5
1	1-1$\frac{3}{4}$ inches	5-10
2	2$\frac{1}{2}$-3 inches	10-20
3	3$\frac{1}{2}$-4 inches	20-25
4	4$\frac{1}{2}$-5 inches	25-30
5	5-6 inches	30
6	6$\frac{1}{4}$-7 inches	>30
Deep water express	7-8 inches	>30
Lead core 450 gr	7-8$\frac{3}{4}$ inches	>30

to a particular depth, use "the countdown method." After making your cast, pull the line straight and begin counting in seconds as the line sinks. For example, a type two line sinks at two and a half to three inches per second; consequently, a forty second count will place the line about ten feet deep.

This countdown method gives you control over the depth that you fish. Know the depth that you want to fish and select the line that will suspend there. A sinking line's suspension property is important because it allows you to present your fly at the desired depth throughout the retrieve. The longer the fly stays where the fish are, the more likely the fish will take it. To some degree, the line selection may be more important than the fly selection. I like to target the submerged weed beds and fish my fly about one or two feet above them.

For most of my still water fishing I use an intermediate sinking line, a type 1 sinking line, or a type 2 sinking line. I find the depths of the submerged weed beds, and then I choose the line that will suspend my fly there.

Sink Tip Lines

A sink tip line is composed of a floating line and a five foot to thirty foot sinking head. Sink tip lines are useful for stream fishing. They present streamers and wet flies well. I seldom use sink tips for nymph fishing because the floating line and strike indicator method is superior. Likewise, I rarely use sink tips in still waters because they seem to create a line arch that makes detecting light strikes difficult.

Sink tips are offered in a wide assortment of lengths and sink rates. I usually prefer the shortest sink tip that will reach the stream's bottom. A convenient way to convert your floating line to a sink tip is to loop on a section of sinking line. Purchase a thirty-foot shooting head in a type four or six density. Cut the head into two foot, three foot, ten foot and fifteen-foot sections. Add loop connections to all section ends. Then simply connect the looped sections to your floating line. By looping together singles and combinations you can create two, three, five, eight, ten, thirteen, fifteen, twenty-five and thirty foot

sink tips. Making your own sink tips saves you from having to buy expensive spare reel spools. All you need is your reel with the floating line, and you have less tackle to carry.

Shooting Heads

I find that shooting heads are useful in salmon, steelhead, and float tube fishing. I prefer a twenty to thirty pound monofilament shooting line. Amnesia is my brand of choice because I can easily straighten out most kinks and coils simply by stretching the line.

Flyfishers can easily make long casts

of 80 to 100 feet by carefully coiling the mono. One or two false casts are all that are needed to propel the line. These shooting heads come in most of the standard line sizes and sink rates. Here I like a line size one or two sizes heavier than my rod's size. Again a wide variety of sink rates allow you to suspend the fly at the desired depths.

Leaders

The leader's purpose is to fool the fish by disguising the fly's connection to the fly line. Flyfishers refer to the end of the leader as the tippet. Line type, water clarity, fish size, and fly size determine the leader's length, taper, flexibility, and strength.

Leaders can become easily kinked from storage on a spool or a reel. The safest

way to straighten leaders is by carefully stretching them with a steady pull. This can be done by pulling the leader between your two hands or by attaching one end of the leader to a stable object and pulling the entire leader at once. Leather coated

rubber straighteners are undesirable because the friction can damage the monofilament and weaken it. Exercise extreme care when using a rubber straightener. Moisten the rubber and pull gently.

Tapered leaders come in knotted or knotless styles. The disadvantage of a knotted tapered leader is that the knots can weaken. Knots can also catch in the guides or attract particles of moss. Coating the knots with Pliobond, Zap a Gap, or Aqua Seal can prevent these problems. The knots can also collect water drops and cause some casting spray. Although such spray is minimal, in extremely placid water conditions it can still become an annoyance. The disadvantage of a tapered knotless leader is that I seem to always buy the ones with a weakened tippet section. Consequently, the first thing that I do after I buy one is to replace the tippet section with a fresh one.

Leaders are attached to the fly line with a well-tied nail knot or a good variation of one. The juncture between fly line and leader is coated with Pliobond, Zap a Gap, or Aqua Seal for smoothness.

Of course, you can tie your own knotted leaders. The advantage of tying your own is that you can custom tie a wide variety of leaders and make them inexpensively. You can make them with very stiff butt materials and super flexible tippets, or you can tie braided butts that are very flexible and use a limp or a stiff tippet. You can also vary the leader's length to meet your specific needs. You will need an assortment of leader sizes and styles.

My favorite knot to join different sized leaders is the triple surgeon's knot. This knot is easier to tie than the blood knot and it doesn't suffer from the uneven wrap that weakens a blood knot. A triple surgeon's knot can also be used to make a loop or a dropper. I like it for tying hard nylon to a soft nylon. I coat this knot with Zap a Gap. Coating the knot prevents the hard nylon from cutting into the softer material and weakening it.

Below you can find a sample list of materials for tying your own custom made leaders:

1. Braided 20 or 30 lb. test Dacron
2. Maxima Ultragreen or Chameleon 25, 20, 18, 15, 10, and 8, lb. test
3. Dai Riki Velvet and Dai Riki standard 0X, 1X, 2X, 3X, 4X, and 5X
4. Fluorocarbon tippet spools in 12,10, 8, and 5 lb. test

Note: Always store leader materials in a dark cool area. When exposed to artificial or sunlight, mono leaders soon deteriorate. Heat can also harm them. When buying tippet spools, select new ones right out of the box or else dig to find one at the bottom of a pile that hasn't been exposed to light. Dark brown monofilaments are more resistant to light damage than clear monofilament. Their shelf life is much longer. My Maxima Chameleon has lasted for years.

Leader Length

The general rule is to select long leaders for floating lines and short leaders for sinking lines. Why? Generally speaking, floating lines disturb the surface film and a long tapered leader is an advantage in placing the fly as far away from the line as possible. On the other hand, sinking lines rarely disturb the surface. They require short leaders because long leaders may buoy up and away from the fish at the desired depth. Sinking lines come in dark bottom colors. Because these colors tend to match the colors of lake and river bottoms and aquatic plants, these leaders tend to go almost unnoticed by fish.

Flexibility

Flexibility is one of a leader's most desirable traits. When trying to provide a naturally drifting fly, the flexibility of the leader buffers the effects of turbulent currents. A stiff leader affects the natural drift of the fly more adversely than a flexible one. Flexibility is critical when fishing upon the surface film.

Try these materials to make a general-purpose leader:

Butt section: stiff German mono (Maxima) about four feet in length
Mid section: use a combination of stiff and flexible material like two feet of Maxima and two feet of Dai Riki
Tippet: about four feet of Dai Riki Velvet

This leader tapers from a stiff butt section to a very limp tippet section. Such a taper transfers the energy of the casting loop progressively to the fly. The leader's long limp tippet protects it from unnatural current drag. (Current drag refers to the pull on a drifting fly and leader made by the current.)

Another leader for even more flexibility in difficult currents consists of the following materials:

Butt section: four feet of braided Dacron
Mid section: four feet of Dai Riki
Tippet section: four feet of Dai Riki Velvet

Because this entire leader is extremely flexible, it is useful for fishing difficult cross currents. The braided butt is very flexible and allows the fly to drift naturally.

Its disadvantage arises when casting the leader in crossing winds: the butt and the remainder of the taper are easily blown off course. This leader's flexibility nevertheless buffers and protects the naturally floating fly from the micro-turbulences of most currents. A cast with some slack laid into it (such as a serpentine cast) can make the leader more productive.

For extreme crosswind conditions, modify the pattern for the general purpose leader by using regular Dai Riki instead of Velvet. A heavier diameter tippet may be substituted for these extreme conditions. For some conditions, you may also want to use the stiff Maxima throughout the leader.

Leaders for strike indicator nymph fishing can be made as follows. Tie the butt section with a highly flexible and thin diameter leader so that it will hinge just below the strike indicator. Keep in mind that the current is always fastest at the surface and progressively decreases in velocity as it nears the stream's bottom. The midsection is further tapered and so is the tippet.

A short section of 0X is useful to attach with a nail knot to the line. The strike indicator is placed on this upper 0X butt section. The length of this leader is varied by changing the length of its midsection. Changing the midsection allows you to adapt your fishing to various depths.

Visibility

Do fish really see leaders and shy away from them, or is it more often an unnaturally moving fly that they avoid, or both? I believe fish notice the drag or unnatural motion imparted to the fly from an unnecessarily stiff leader rather than the visibility of the leader. The late Charles Brooks's experiment using highly visible size A white winding thread as a tippet supports this theory. So called "leader shy fish" readily took Mr. Brooks's fly when he fished it with size A thread. The thread was highly visible, but it was extremely flexible.

The new fluorocarbon leaders interest me. Underwater they seem to disappear. Consequently, I can get away with using a heavy leader, which is an advantage in fighting a fish. A loop knot tied to attach the fly to the tippet allows the fly excellent freedom of movement. Perhaps their other advantage is that fluorocarbon leaders are denser than monofilament leaders and inherently sink. A floating leader seems to disturb the surface film because its movements reflect light and cause waves. A sunken leader does not disturb the surface. In short, when fishing for highly educated trout I opt for either a long flexible tippet or a fluorocarbon tippet with a loop knotted fly.

Sinking line leaders are simply three to five foot sections of tippet slightly tapered and attached to about one foot of heavy leader attached to the fly line. Leader Test: A leader's "test" refers to its relative strength and size.

I prefer to use heavier tippets than most other fishermen. I like to forcibly fight my fish so that they can be quickly released unharmed by fatigue. I get away with heavier tippets by using a very flexible material such as Dai Riki Velvet or a fluorocarbon tippet with a loop knot fly attachment. My tippets generally average about four feet in length. This system gives me adequate strength for fighting fish, pulling out snags, and abrasion resistance.

The general rule about leader length is occasionally broken when fishing sinking lines in lakes that are weed infested. Under these conditions, I use a long leader that buoys upwards somewhat and allows me to retrieve line out of the thick weed beds. I also use a slightly faster sink rate line than ordinarily needed with this long leader. The buoyed fly is pulled downward during the retrieve; likewise the fly buoys upwards during the pause. The faster sinking line gets my fly down quickly and saves time. The rise and fall of the fly is an effective retrieve. A slightly buoyant fly pattern accentuates this motion. Flies tied with deer hair such as Werner shrimp and Muddler minnows are effective. The leader length I use varies between 8 and 10 feet.

When fishing a dry fly, I lessen water splash due to casting by using a longer than normal leader. Fifteen-foot leaders carry fewer water droplets and are useful in very calm, clear water conditions. They make transparent false casting above the fish less noticeable and less likely to cause alarm. Lake fishing with midges and a floating line may require extraordinarily long leaders. When retrieved towards the surface, these long leaders permit flyfishers to imitate the slow ascent of midge pupa. The extreme

lengths allow these leaders to sink to the bottom.

Loop to loop leader connections are popular because they facilitate easy and fast changes to a new or different sized tippet. Their disadvantage is that the loops may hang up a fly cast with a tailing loop.

Wind knots severely weaken leaders. When I discover one, I replace the wind knotted section of the leader or untie the wind knot if it hasn't yet pulled tight.

The butt section needs to be a next size lower than fly line diameter. Leaders taper towards the tippet in progressively finer diameters to permit the casting loop to unfurl the leader on delivery.

Heavily wind resistant flies call for stiffer materials to straighten out the leader. Casting a tight loop increases the fly's momentum by increasing the line speed. Small flies require smaller diameter and more flexible leaders to cast properly.

It's best to become a proficient caster: a well cast leader will always straighten upon delivery. Controlling line speed and loop

size are important casting skills. The most demanding conditions are those of crystal clear waters with smooth surface flows and mini current disturbances caused by weeds and minor obstructions. Fishing the surface under these conditions demands the most from a leader. You can overcome these adversarial conditions by using as flexible a leader as possible. A stiff leader causes the fly to float unnaturally.

I like my leaders to sink just under the surface. When leaders float, they disturb the surface by reflecting light and causing ripples. Leader sink products are useful, and so are techniques like pre-wetting the leader prior to casting or rubbing mud or weed slime on the leader. Just prior to fishing, you can also soak a leader in a water-filled zip lock bag.

Backing

The backing is an added braided line that connects the reel's spool to the ordinary fly line. Since fly lines average 75-115 feet in length, the lines require backing for those times when a large fish runs out all of the regular fly line. Without backing, you would quickly part ways.

Small waters rarely require much backing; usually fifty yards is adequate. In larger waters, at least 100 yards of backing is needed. If a fish runs out more than 100 yards, your chances of landing it are slim. Saltwater species require 200 to 600 yards of backing. In the open ocean, however, there is less chance that the fish may wrap up line around a rock or a log.

I prefer twenty pound braided Dacron for fresh water conditions and thirty pound braided Dacron for saltwater conditions. I prefer the braided Dacron because its diameter is larger than the new Spectra lines. Thin Spectra lines can cut into the spool of backing and jam; this usually causes a big fish to be lost. Flyfishers use an arbor knot to connect the backing to the spool. The fly line/backing connection requires an Albright knot.

Vests

A vest helps organize your tackle by spreading the weight and the bulk evenly around your upper body. The vest's back pocket can hold a light rain jacket and refreshments. A heavily loaded vest, however, is cumbersome and restricts casting movements. Pack only the items that you really use. Keep the rest of the tackle inside the car.

Deep wading and float tube fishing may flood a vest's lower pockets. In cold weather, a vest can become even more constrictive when worn over heavy clothing. Instead, I prefer a chest pack to a vest. My chest pack is well balanced and holds about everything that I really need. A chest pack also slips easily over your shoulders and carries the equipment balanced on your chest and back. Chest packs also permit plenty of arm and shoulder movements, and they keep your gear out of the water when float tubing and deep wading. There is a wide assortment of chest packs on the market, although you should stay away from the ones that protrude excessively because they can restrict your vision by obscuring your feet, causing you to stumble or even to fall over an unseen rock or branch.

Polarized Glasses

Polarized glasses are a "must have" item. With them on you can see straight into the water to spot fish and underwater structures. They also protect your eyes from harmful ultra-violet rays and errantly cast flies.

Polarized glasses are best worn with a cap with black bill on the underneath side. The dark underside of the hat's bill lessens the reflected glare and gives you your best vision. Cutting down on the amount of reflected light results in less eye fatigue.

In bright conditions, amber, gray, or green lenses work well. For low light, a yellow lens is best. Because I fish more during low light, I use my yellow lenses the most.

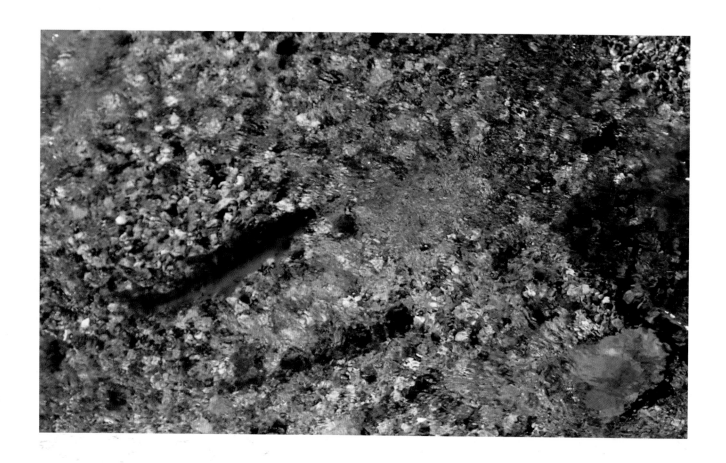

Other Equipment

1. Knippers: these take up little space and easily cut leaders.
2. Scissor Plier Combination: handy for de-barbing hooks, removing flies, and for cutting leaders.
3. Small Tube: assists in tying nail knots.
4. Fly Boxes: choose lightweight, closed cell foam boxes that close tightly. These will float.
5. Magnification: a pair of drug store magnifying glasses helps us mature anglers tie better knots.
6. Rod cases: use the ones that protect both the rod and the reel from damage.

CASTING 2

Casting Grip

The casting grip is made by placing the thumb extended over the top of the rod's cork grip. The index finger is directly underneath the thumb with the middle ring finger and little fingers lending support by gripping the cork between the entire thumb and these fingers. The greatest gripping strength is made between the thumb and the index and middle fingers. The ring and little finger have a somewhat more relaxed grasp. Nearly opposite each other are the thumb and index fingers which are seated in the cork's walls.

The wrist is stiff, while the elbow is loose. The rod becomes an extension of your forearm. Consequently, the shoulder and elbow joints control the rod's movements. For example: this grip is similar to holding a hammer and nailing a spike. The wrist is locked and doesn't move during the casting stroke.

Power Stroke

The power stroke is made with a locked wrist similar to hammering a nail. The forearm does most of the movement while the wrist is immobile. The elbow passes through a horizontal plane as if on an imaginary fence rail during both the forward and backcasts. This motion generates tighter casting loops. It is the most efficient stroke. On the backcast the wrist is also locked. For most short casts use a shorter casting stroke, but for powerful and long casts use a longer casting stroke.

The backcast is made using a hammering or a stabbing motion. This stabbing enhances the strength of the backcast.

The power stroke is a smooth accelerated motion ending in a sudden stop. The acceleration starts slowly and progresses faster until it peaks at the abrupt stop. This stop transfers the energy to the line. Most people are strong forward casters but weak backcasters; similarly, racquet sports players often suffer from the same problem of weak backhand strokes.

Backcast

1. Start the backcast with the rod butt as close as possible to your forearm wrist region. This means your wrist is slanted in a bent down position. A successful backcast requires the line to be straight in order to get it moving. Simply retrieve the line and do not start the backcast stroke until the line is straightened.

2. The wrist remains locked and the forearm stabs the rod backwards turning the rod over and creating a line loop. Tight backcast and forward cast loops are created with the elbow traveling in a horizontal plane; otherwise, wide loops are made by arching the elbow's path. The longest cast demands the tightest loops. Tight loops result in maximum line speeds which travel longer distances.

3. At the end of the backcast stroke your rod hand should be behind your shoulder. Allow the line to straighten before starting the forward cast. Remember the line must first be straight before it can be moved.

Forward Cast

1. Aim for a specific target. Picture the distance between your hand and the target. Push your wrist and thumb directly in a stroke towards the target. The thumb's path is the direction that the line will follow.

2. To complete the forward cast, drive forward with the forearm rotating from the shoulder and the elbow joint. Again the wrist joint must be locked. This power stroke is made by smooth acceleration and by a sudden stop at the end of the casting stroke. The forward cast sweeps the rod forward throughout a long arc. Tight loops are created by having your elbow travel through a straight horizontal path.

Overall Tips, Points and Advice

1. The casting stroke is a smooth accelerated movement ending in a sudden stop. At first, the rod is accelerated slowly; then it smoothly increases until the power stroke ends with an abrupt stop.

2. At all times the line must be straight to be cast. The forward cast starts when the line is straightened by the backcast. All slack coils have to be eliminated before you can get the end of the line moving.

3. Observe how the line unrolls during all casting strokes. A caster's goal is to control loop size, line speed, and direction.

Summary Points

1. The smooth acceleration with an abrupt stop is essential to the casting stroke. Tight loops are created by having the elbow pass through a straight horizontal path. Wide loops are made by making an arc in the elbow's path. Tight loops are faster and more aerodynamic than wide loops; they allow for longer casts. On the other hand, wide loops are slower and delicate. Wide loops are used at times when a delicate delivery is needed. But most of the time a tight loop cast is best. It's imperative to develop a smoothly accelerated stroke by passing the elbow through a straight horizontal path. Finally the casting stroke ends in an abrupt stop.

2. Forearm movement is made from the elbow and shoulder joint for both back and forward casts. This motion is similar to driving a nail with a hammer. Visualize a double headed hammer used to pound nails on both the back and forward strokes. This same smooth acceleration stroke that efficiently drives a nail drives the cast. THE SUDDEN STOP TRANSFERS ALL OF THE ENERGY TO THE LINE.

3. Clock positions: long casts correspondingly require longer rod arc strokes than shorter casts. Many short casts can be made between the 1 and 11 o'clock positions, while longer casts are between the 3 and 9 o'clock positions. Conserve your energy when casting by not expending any more motion than is necessary.

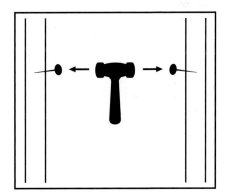

Physical Conditioning

Weight training exercises can help develop casting muscles. These muscles can be developed through a program of resistance training. Gripping a long handled ax or sledge hammer like a rod and lifting it in sets of repetitions can develop these casting muscles.

Perform 3 to 6 sets of 12 reps every other day for about 6 weeks. As strength develops use more resistance by increasing distance between ax head and wrist.

Good casters have powerful power strokes and well-conditioned muscles. It requires wrist strength to keep the wrist motionless.

In addition, dumbbell training may help condition forearm casting muscles. Exercise the muscles used in the casting strokes motion by lying prone on a weight bench, and then while leaning over the bench lift the dumbbell in the backcast stroke. Forward cast muscles are developed by placing your back on the bench and reversing the exercise. Again, 3 to 6 sets of 12 reps are performed 3 times a week for at least 6 weeks. Increase resistance as strength develops.

False Casting

False casting is a series of forward and backcasts that do not allow the line to fall on the forward cast position. Hence, the forward cast is treated as just another backcast. Its purpose is to establish both length and direction for casting accuracy. False casting increases distance and floating properties. It dries off the fly improving its floating properties.

The basic 10 to 2 o'clock casting strokes are made reversing their directions when the line is about straight. If the casting stroke is made prior to line straightening an annoying whipping action occurs.

Tailing Loop/Sudden Stop

A tailing loop is one that drops the upper line down to intersect the lower line. Occurring on either the forward or backcast, tailing loops are undesirable because casting efficiency is lost and tangles and wind knots are created. Simply, the tailing loop loses casting momentum and doesn't straighten the line.

An improper acceleration of the casting stroke creates most tailing loops. Mine are made when I suddenly start the cast with too fast of an acceleration and then slow the acceleration rate before the stop.

Correcting a tailing loop is done by performing the casting stroke with smooth acceleration capped off with a sudden stop. This sudden stop sends the line to flow out in an even roll.

Stop

The quickness of the stop influences both line speed and loop size. Slow stops create open loops with slow speeds; however, sudden stops create narrow loops with high speeds.

The slow stop is made when the caster flings his arms out in a futile attempt to gain distance. It's like trying to push a rope. Releasing the rod's stored energy all at once by making an abrupt stop propels the line efficiently in a tight casting loop.

The caster conserves energy by casting with smooth controlled acceleration and by stopping hard. This makes the rod do most of the work by flexing and releasing its potential energy all at once. For example: a bicyclist accelerates fast and hits a wall; the bike comes to a sudden stop throwing its rider into the wall. On the other hand, if the bike comes to a slow stop and merely bumps the wall the rider is hardly displaced.

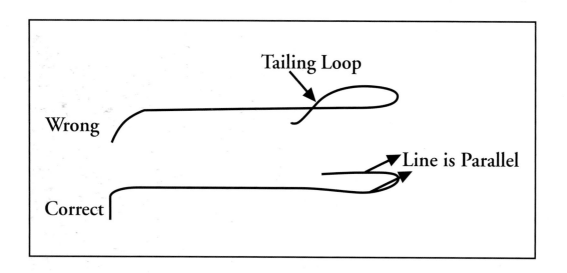

Follow Through

The follow through comes after the hard stop segment of the cast. It is done to keep tension on the bottom leg of the loop so that the line will fire out at a fast speed. Releasing this line tension slows the cast down. The loop doesn't unroll because the lower loop segment needs to be held in tension. Without tension the loop's energy is lost and the cast fails. So hold tight to the bottom leg of the loop to enhance casting efficiency.

Increasing bottom leg tension by drawing back or slightly lifting the rod tip boosts the line speed. For instance cracking a whip demands a pulling back motion as the whip unrolls. In casting, follow through by holding back line tension to greatly improve casting speed and distance.

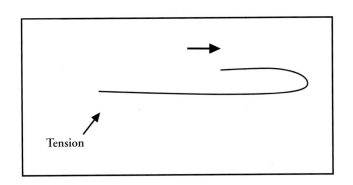

Single Haul

A simple way to perform the single haul cast is to grasp the line and to hold it stationary downwards at your side during the backcast. The rod hand movement pulls the line back as it moves through the backcast stroke. (See Diagram 1)

This is a very efficient casting method. In a timely manner the line is pulled back automatically on the backcast; it enhances the backcast by increasing its line speed. Backcasts are weaker than forward casts, and the single haul helps strengthen the backcast.

A true single haul takes this pulling back on the line during the backcast one step further by having the line hand pull down at the same time as the backcast stroke is made. Additional line momentum is created giving the backcast higher line speed. Remember the line must be straightened out before it can be cast; a straightened backcast line is easier to cast on the forward cast. (See Diagram 2.)

I use one of these single hauls on every cast because it greatly improves my backcast. This haul is timed to occur during the last half of the casting stroke. It is a short fast downward pull by the line hand that complements the smooth acceleration stroke.

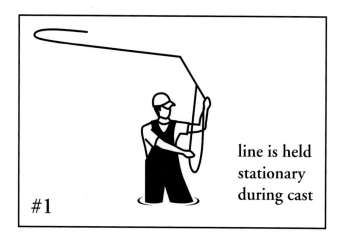

line is held
stationary
during cast

#1

pull down to
make the
single haul

#2

Double Haul

The double haul cast includes the single haul on the backcast plus an additional haul on the forward cast. Its purpose is to increase line speed and momentum for distance. Besides, some line can be shot on the backcast so when it straightens out the additional forward haul can shoot even more line on the forward cast.

Again, the same single haul is made on the backcast and the forward cast haul is made as follows: The line hand on the forward cast abruptly pulls the line downwards towards the thigh as the forearm casting stroke progresses. The line is released just after the power strokes stop; furthermore, the line is shot to the target. (See Diagram 3) This haul must be timed to occur during the last half of the casting stroke. It is used to enhance the smooth acceleration. If the haul is done prematurely a tailing loop may be created.

The double haul cast provides the fastest line speeds and longest distances. For casting in the wind and casting shooting heads, the double haul cast is ideal. (See Diagram 4)

#3

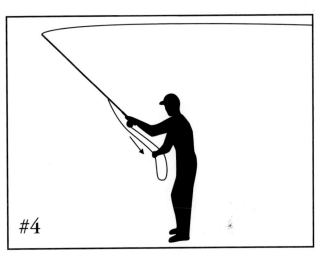

#4

Type of Casts

Backhand Cast

The backhand cast is useful for casting on the opposite side of your body. Instead of switching the rod from the dominant hand to the other hand, the dominant hand is employed throughout the cast. Most right handed casters have difficulty casting left handed. Many times a wind or an obstruction limits one-sided casting; for example, a stiff breeze blown onto the right side of a right handed caster blows the line onto the caster. It's corrected by either casting left handed or by using this backhand cast. Also, an obstruction like a tree on your right side limits your casting stroke from being completely done on your left side.

Remaining on the caster's dominant side, the rod is raised over the head high enough and tilted so the casting planes are performed across. The rod tip and line now pass on your backhand side. A normal casting stroke is used except the rod hand

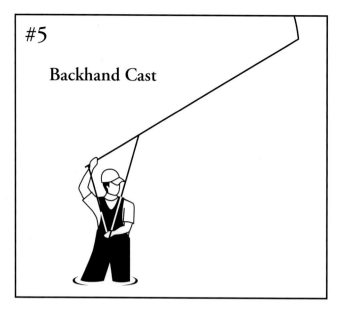

#5

Backhand Cast

position is one that's similar to brushing your hair. Away from your body the line passes safely, although sloppy casts and some widened loops may pass the line close to your body. (See Diagram 5)

The backhand cast is ideal for avoiding both wind and obstructions on your casting hand's side.

Reach Cast

The reach cast is perhaps the most useful cast for stream fishing. It provides

an aerial mend which enhances a drag free drift.

Simply, the reach cast is made just after the forward cast stops by reaching the rod into the direction that you want the line belly to travel. Keep enough tension on back of the loop so it maintains enough momentum to reposition the line belly. The power stroke's hard stop directs the loops towards the target. Only the line belly close to the caster is redirected. (See Diagram 6) The final forward cast should be aimed slightly higher and somewhat overpowered than usual. These modifications enhance the fly's ability to reach the target and cause the line belly to be favorably repositioned. As the line straightens out in front of you, keep the rod tip held high above your head. Just as the line begins to turn over, reach the rod into the desired direction. Reach as far as you can, then simultaneously drop the rod tip and line to the water.

An upstream reach cast is useful when casting from fast to slower currents.

In summary, the reach cast is simply an aerial mend allowing the line belly to land in a more favorable location to enhance a longer drag free float.

Tuck Cast

The tuck cast is used for drag free floats in difficult eddies and for quickly sinking a weighted fly; consequently, in the tuck cast the fly lands first with the leader heaped up on top of it.

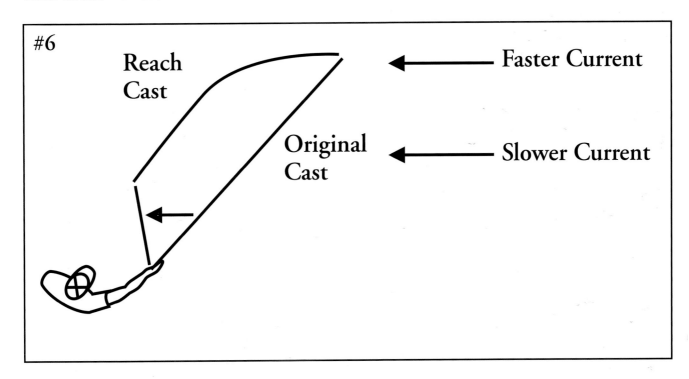

#6

Reach Cast

Original Cast

Faster Current

Slower Current

Simply, the tuck cast is made by overpowering a higher-than-normal forward cast by abruptly stopping it. Put some speed into the tight looped cast, so the fly turns over and then under the leader, landing the fly first. The slacked leader piled onto the fly allows the fly to sink freely and to drift longer without drag.

Wind resistant bushy flies are awkward to turn over, but the tuck cast readily turns over sparsely tied flies. (See Diagram 7)

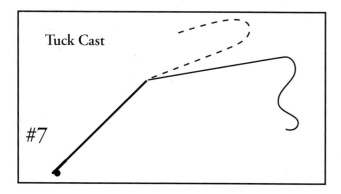

Roll Cast

The roll cast is useful when you lack the open space for a backcast. Instead of making a backcast, build momentum by rolling the line in an over motion that replaces the backcast stroke.

To perform the roll cast, the rod is smoothly lifted back to the backcasting stroke (9:00 or 10:00 o'clock position) by slowly moving the line. The line is straightened and a widened loop is formed. While it still lies on the water's surface, power this loop forward by a casting stroke which energizes the loop into unrolling and making a lengthened cast. The same forward cast is made complete with a short, smooth, accelerating, straight elbow path,

and a sudden stop. The only modification is the gentle backcast stroke designed to straighten the line and to form a wide loop. (See Diagram 8) Remember to draw the loop far back from your shoulder.

It's best to practice the roll cast on water; a grass surface creates line drag that dampens the cast.

Sidearm Casting

Sidearm casting is useful for fishing in windy conditions and for casting under overhanging vegetation. Additionally, it's helpful in avoiding other anglers when fishing from restricted areas such as a drift boat. Since wind and overhanging vegetation is ubiquitous, the sidearm cast is frequently used.

Sidearm casting readily throws a curved line and leader; furthermore, such a curved cast is useful in reducing the effects of drag. Both positive and negative curves can be created. Positive curves are created by overpowering the sidearm casting stroke; negative curves are caused by under powering the delivery. In addition, a hard stop can create a positive curve, and a soft stop can make a negative curve.

The sidearm cast uses the same casting strokes and principals as the overhead cast; these strokes are just completed on a tilted side plane.

Wind has less velocity the closer it approaches the water and ground. In these leeward areas the sidearm cast is more efficient. Sidearm casting in these lower areas of less wind results in efficient casting. Also, a sidearm cast can place the fly underneath an overhanging tree branch to reach a prime lie.

Different degrees of sidearm casting can be employed. I use a slight degree during all of my overhead casts because it keeps the false cast fly 6-8 feet safely away from me. I continually employ the sidearm cast at windy times and at covered areas.

Wind Casting

Along with the sidearm cast there are some other tips for casting on windy days. Use the tightest fastest loops that you can cast because they are less wind resistant. Also, I prefer to cast smaller diameter lines. Once I fished my two wt. outfit on an extremely windy day on the lower Henry's Fork River. I was amazed at how well it performed. My favorite windy day outfit is a fast action 4 wt. rod and a 4 wt. line. With this outfit I can create narrow fast loops which cut through the wind more

effectively than my 7 and 8 weight outfits. I guess it's easier to toss a softball than a volley ball on a windy day.

Angle the casting planes to take advantage of the wind. For example, when casting into the wind angle the backcast high where the wind will help straighten it out; then, direct the forward cast downwards toward the surface where there is less wind. (See Diagram 9)

Casting with the wind aids the forward cast and hinders the backcast. Since the line must be straightened before it can be cast, restrict the backcast to shorter lengths and shoot more line on the forward cast. Again, angle the shortened backcast low into the wind and angle the forward cast up higher to use the wind to help shoot the line.

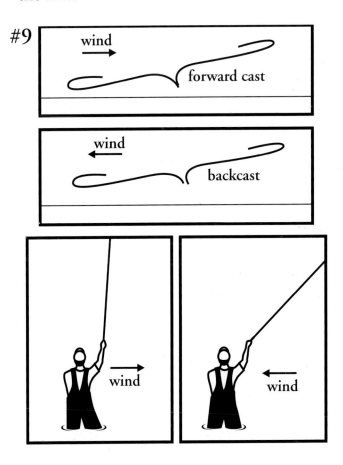

#9

Unsnagging Roll Cast

The unsnagging roll cast is used in an attempt to pull against a snagged fly from the opposite direction.

Once snagged, pull some additional line out and overpower a roll cast forcing the line to roll in back of the snagged fly. Then make a quick forceful backcast stroke which enhances this backwards pull. Hopefully these two motions will dislodge the fly. If successful, inspect the hook and tippet for damage. (See Diagram 10)

This unsnagging roll cast works some of the time, but many snagged flies are just too securely hooked and will be lost.

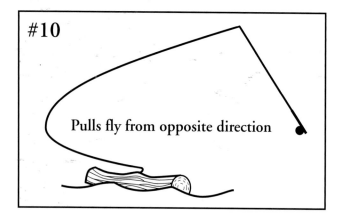

#10
Pulls fly from opposite direction

Posture (Body Position)

To provide the longest possible casting arcs the caster's body is angled sideward toward the target. The foot opposite the casting arm is placed in the forward position pointed at the target. The other foot is placed behind and turned outwards nearly at a right angle from the line of cast. (See Diagram 11) On the forward cast the body weight is shifted to the forward foot; likewise on the backcast the weight is shifted to the back foot. In this stance the caster can easily view the backcast by turning the head. This body position allows for maximum rod arc movement needed for maximum distance casting. This stance allows the rod hand to drift backwards and upwards on the backcast.

This drift occurs after the backcast is completed and allows for a longer forward cast stroke. (See Diagram 12)

#11

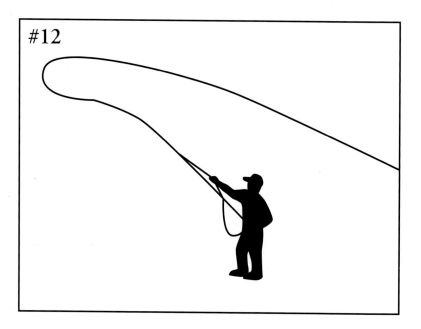

#12

Distance Casting Trajectories

For distance casting, angle the trajectories so it is launched upwards on both the back and forward casts. When the line straightens it will settle to a lower angle. Start both forward and back casts at this lowered angle. These trajectories allow for maximum casting distances because the rod moves through the longest possible arc. (See Diagram 13)

#13   forward cast   backcast

Wiggle Cast

The slack line cast is useful to promote a drag free float across complex currents. Its purpose is to lay out the line and leader in a serpentine manner causing a prolonged drift to occur as the currents unravel the coils.

The wiggle cast is useful in upstream, across stream, and downstream presentations. Easy to do, the wiggle cast is performed by wiggling the rod just after the forward cast power stroke. Keep slight tension on the line. The rod wiggling is done in the horizontal plane. When properly performed, the fly is sent on target with the leader and line lying down in a snakelike pattern. Slightly elevating the forward cast's trajectory and slowing down the line speed gives more time to wiggle even more slack line coils.

Fly Fishing: *The Lifetime Sport*   **41**

Practice Methods

Perhaps the most effective practice method is to start with the amount of line that you can cast efficiently. Practice casting perfect loops on both the back and forward casts. In addition learn to adjust the loop size on command. Once you are proficient casting at a short line length, gradually increase the distance in about 5 foot increments. The technical demands grow as you increase the casting distance. With time you will be casting a long line with ease.

Hula hoop practice is good for both accuracy and loop control. Prop one up vertically and practice casting a narrow loop through the hoop. To develop accuracy, lay the hoops down at different distances and practice placing the fly inside the hoops.

Target practice also helps develop accuracy. Try casting to the edge of the flower garden, or underneath a tree. Place tennis balls out on the lawn at various distances and cast to them. Again the hula hoops make good targets, but my mind is programmed to cast to the edge of them and not to their midst. I enjoy casting to our pet cat; cats get excited and love to play with the yarn fly. In practice, cast to the cat just as if it was a fish. Lay the yarn down gently in front of the cat and watch its excitement in pouncing on the yarn. The cat provides a moveable target with lots of odd angles. Plus it relishes the activity. Cast gently so the cat will not be harmed. Use a tuft of soft yarn tied onto the leader. Pretend the cat is a willing fish ready to take a properly presented fly.

Another practice goal is to perfect your casting using as little energy expenditure as possible. Rely upon exact timing, coordinating accelerations, short casting strokes and sudden stops to make the rod do most of the work. With time the rod will be like an extension of your arm and it will amaze you how effortlessly you can cast.

During practice sessions place emphasis on the power stroke and stop. These are the critical movements needed for good casting technique.

For improving distance, practice shooting as much line as possible. Shoot line on the backcast. The backcast is the weakest casting stroke. By learning to shoot line on the backcast you must perfect its line speed and tight narrow loop control; likewise, cast shooting line on the forward cast.

Small targets, such as a cup or a loaded mousetrap, are good practice. You must precisely cast to set off the trap or to place the fly inside the cup.

Fly casting is similar to basketball. With repetitive practice, distance and accuracy skills are learned. Daily practice sessions lead to success; without practice, casting perfection is not possible.

My most enjoyable practice sessions occur on the stream when casting to real fish. Try to perfect your casting skills on a week's fishing trip.

Wind Direction In Your Face

When casting into the wind, correct the forward cast by tilting the loop somewhat towards the water; likewise, orient the backcast above its usual plane. Drive the forward cast hard into the wind by using a tight casting loop. (See Diagram 14)

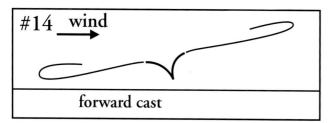

Wind On Your Back

When casting with the wind, over power the backcast and drive it below the usual casting plane; likewise, cast the forward cast above its normal plane.

The forward cast is benefited by the wind. Also, orienting the backcast lower reduces the effect of the wind by taking advantage of buffered wind close to the ground. Employ a tight fast loop on the back cast; furthermore, shoot line on the foreword cast and let the wind help carry it out.

Crosswinds

Crosswinds complicate casting. In Diagram 15 a wind blows the line onto the caster's body. This presents a handicap because the casting stroke can pass the fly dangerously close to your body. Compensate by making shorter casts or if possible repositioning yourself across the stream where the wind blows the casting line away from you. The position of the caster is an advantage because the casting planes are directed away from your body

and the backcast stroke doesn't cross your body.

Additionally, crosswinds complicate a natural drift and require additional line mending. Reach casts are useful in cross winds.

Circle Cast

The circle cast is used for casting when the wind blows the line back onto your body. Both the forward and the backcasts are made with the rod held high over your head and with the casting planes oriented towards your downwind side. This allows the casting line to safely travel away from your body. This casting plane is assisted by the wind, making it travel somewhat in a circle. (See Diagram 16)

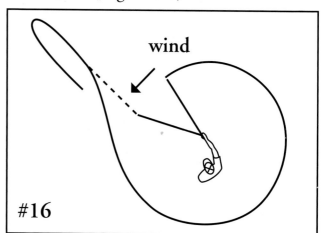

Off Hand Casting

Being able to cast with both hands is a blessing. In a crosswind, simply, switch hands to cast on the other side. It is difficult to cast accurately and far away with the weak hand. Windy conditions favor a closer approach. Short casts are easier to control and require less mending.

Backwards Cast

The backwards cast delivers the fly on the backcast. It is mechanically the same as the standard overhead cast; simply look over your shoulder and present the fly on the backcast. (See Diagram 17)

In summary, crosswind casting can be accomplished in a variety of ways. Increase line speeds by casting narrow loops by using single and double haul casts.

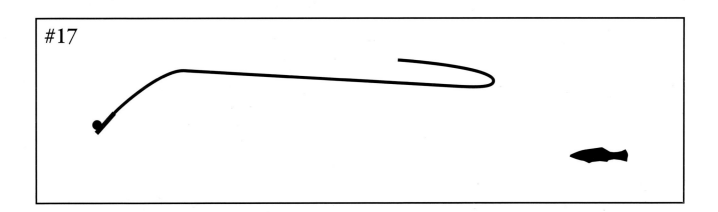

#17

AQUATIC FOODS

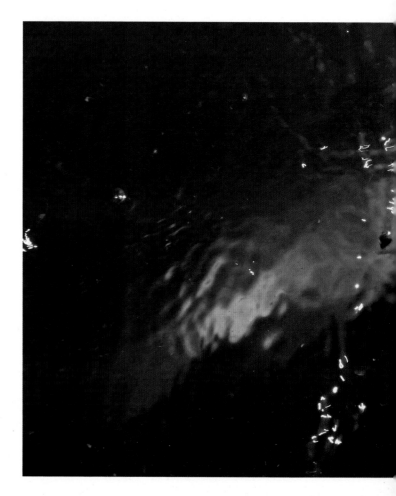

Fish feed upon a great variety of water and land born nourishments. An angler's artificial flies are designed to imitate these foods. Matching your fly to the specific fare that the fish are presently feeding upon is the key to success.

Land born foods are classified as terrestrials and water born foods are classified as aquatics. The significant terrestrials are ants, grasshoppers, mice, moths, lizards, earthworms, beetles, and crickets. The important aquatics are caddisflies, mayflies, stoneflies, midges, craneflies, dragonflies, damselflies, crustaceans, forage fish, leeches and eels.

These natural foods can be imitated by today's flies. But first the natural food must be identified.

Knowledge of what the fish are presently feeding upon is essential to select the right fly. Time spent observing before fishing is well spent.

Start by watching the water's surface for insect activity. Observe both the birds and the fish to see what they are feeding upon. I carry a pair of compact binoculars and use them often. Then I collect a sample insect.

A small aquarium net can help collect the insects. Place the net just under the water's surface to catch the actively hatching insects. Also use the net to catch the airborne ones. Find a spider's web and observe its contents for it contains a history of the available insects. A stomach pump can remove the fish's recently ingested food. But first a fish must be caught. The pump is sold in most fly shops and is designed for its intended purpose. It is simply a rubber bulb with a plastic tube. Squeezing the bulb injects a small amount of water into the fish's stomach; next the pressure on the pump is released sucking some of the fish's ingested food back into the bulb. Then squeeze the bulb's contents back into your hand or into a white container. Inspect the contents. A major disadvantage is that the pump only removes the small food items and not the large ones lodged in the stomach. The pump's advantage is you can identify the small presently ingested insects.

A large screen is useful in identifying the assortment of foodstuffs in a stream. Such knowledge is useful when purchasing or tying flies for the specific stream. The screen is made by stapling a three foot section of window screen to two broom handles or one inch by two inch slat boards. Place the screen downstream from your waded position. Next, dislodge or overturn rocks with your feet and allow the debris to collect onto the screen. Take the screen ashore and examine its contents. It will contain a large sample of the stream's aquatic foods. Save its contents in small bottles filled with eighty percent alcohol and twenty percent water.

Once the foodstuff is collected, try to identify it. Next, go through your fly box and make a match. Choose a fly that mimics the foodstuff's size, texture, color and shape. Imitate the food's action with the proper presentation and retrieve.

The size means the foodstuff's measurements in terms of thickness, width, and length. Foods smaller than a half inch are best imitated as to their exact length; on the other hand, foods larger than a half inch are best imitated as to its exact width. Choose your fly selection accordingly.

The *texture* is the overall feel as to the food's softness or rigidity. A fish's mouth readily detects texture and a too soft or too hard fly will be readily rejected while a good match will be ingested.

The *shape* is the food's silhouette. This outline is an important consideration in matching the fly. Suggestive and impressionistic flies that match the foodstuff's three dimensional shape are the most successful. Suggestive flies can match a multitude of possible foods while exact imitations sometimes restrict the number of matches.

The *color* match is helpful but it is not as important as the other elements of imitation. Natural food's color and patterns can vary in shades and tones. Select your fly as to the general color pattern of the natural.

Action is the foodstuff's natural movement. The presentation and the retrieve mimics this motion. Action depicts a living movement that fish key upon while feeding.

An outline of the foodstuffs will be presented. Volumes of text could be written on the huge variety of foodstuffs eaten by fish. There are thousands of varieties of both land born and stream born insects. Try to classify your findings into one of the following general groups. Match the natural food's size, texture, color, action, and silhouette with one of your flies.

Mayflies

Order: Ephemeroptera
Life Cycle: incomplete
Three Life Stages: egg-aquatic nymph, and
 adult cycle which includes two phases:
 (subimago) dun and (imago stage) spinner
Species: over one thousand
Hatch is over a one to three week period
 yearly

Mayflies undergo an incomplete metamorphosis, meaning that typically in a one year period they go through three cycles: egg, nymph and adults. Most of the mayfly's life is spent in the nymphal cycle.

There are four different groups that the mayflies are divided into depending on body type and behavior. These are: burrowers, clingers, crawlers and swimmers. Burrowers have an oval, long-shaped body with fringed gills and very visible tusk-like mandibles. The clinger mayfly has a head wider than the abdomen and a flattened body. Crawlers have a head equal to, or less than, the width of the abdomen and have a slightly flattened body. Along the top margin of the abdomen are forked gills; except for a few species they have no tusk-like mandibles. The round, streamlined body of the swimmer has a head equal to, or less than the width of its abdomen. Swimmers have tails where the edges are fringed with fine hair.

Nymphs grow as they molt 20 to 30 times and their wing pads darken as their wings start to develop. As the mayfly nymphs start to emerge, most of them swim or drift to the surface and emerge as adult mayflies. Some of the mayfly nymphs emerge under the water and must swim to the surface, or they may crawl out to the shore and hatch.

The adult mayfly goes through 2 phases. The first is a dun and the second phase is commonly called a spinner. The newly hatched adults are called duns and fly to the steam's foliage after emergence. In this dun phase the adults are unable to mate and have opaque wings. The spinner emerges anywhere from one hour to 3 days after the dun sheds its outer covering. The sexually mature spinners have clear wings and form mating swarms in the air. When a female comes into the swarm she is seized by a male and mating takes place. After mating, the male usually falls spent to the water or ground and the female begins depositing her eggs on the water's surface or sometimes underneath the water. Then she falls spent, creating a spinner's fall. Trout enjoy most of the phases of the different 4 groups, having interest in some more than others.

Mayflies

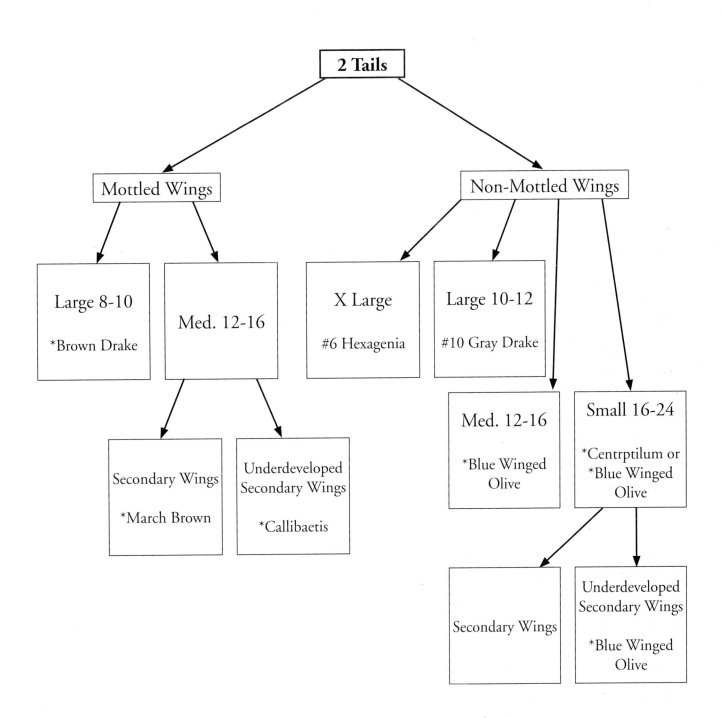

Mayflies

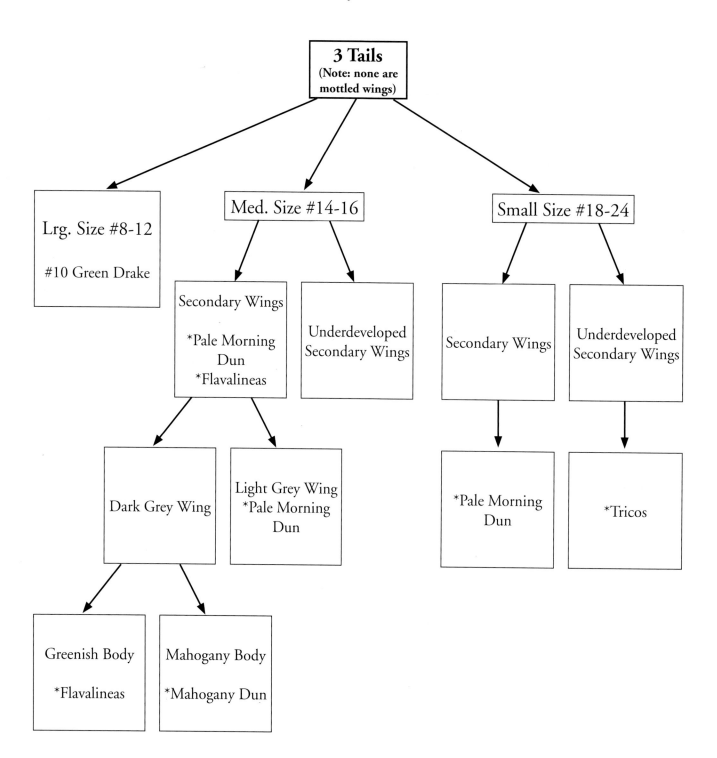

Mahogany Dun

Family: Leptophlebiidae
Genus: Paraleptophlebia
Life Cycle: incomplete
Three Life Stages: egg, nymph, adult
    cycle which includes 2 phases: dun
    and spinner
Emergence: August-October

Nymph

Body Description
Antennae: 2, longer
Head: sickle-shaped tusks on head
Abdomen: single tuning-fork
    gills on abdomen
Tails: 3
Legs: 6
Body Color: olive-brown to
    dark brown
Mobility: not strong crawlers
Size: 7-9mm
Hook Size: 12-16

More available to fish in small to medium streams; although a larger population can be common in bigger streams.

Dun

Body Description
Antennae: 2, short
Wings: 2 sets with hind wings
    being rounded, gray slate
    color
Tails: 3
Legs: 6
Body Color: reddish-brown
Size: 7-9mm
Hook Size: 12-16

Spinner

Spinners are not covered
because of the lack of spinners
falling on the water and no interest from
    the trout.

Pale Morning Dun

Family: Ephemerelidae
Genus: Ephemerella
Life Cycle: incomplete
Three Life Stages: egg, nymph, adult cycle
    which includes 2 phases: dun and
    spinner
Emergence: May-August
Crawler Mayfly Group

Nymph

Body Description
Antennae: 2
Legs: 6
Tails: 3
Wings: none
Body Colors: olive brown
Mobility: swim slowly, not very
    active

**Live among the rocks and debris in runs,
flats or riffles in spring creeks, tail
waters, or freestone streams.**

Dun

Body Description
Antennae: 2
Legs: 6
Tails: 3
Wings: 2 sets-hind wings well developed
    (always pale grey), rounded projection
    of leading edge of back wings; hind
    wings are well developed. This
    distinguishes them from blue wing
    olives which are very small
Eyes: overly large

Body Colors: light olive, pale yellow,
    bright yellow, tannish olive, orange,
    olive brown
Mobility: on overcast days after
    emergence they spend more time
    on the water
Size: 7-9mm
Hook Size: 14-16

Spinner

Body Description
Antennae: 2
Legs: 6
Tails: 3
Wings: 2 sets, transparent
Eyes: large
Body Colors: have darker bodies
    than duns which are brown with
    yellow-olive tones
Size: 7-9mm
Hook Size: 14-16

**Females fly into swarms to mate while in
flight. Males fall spent into the water
while the females fly to choppy water
and deposit their eggs after which
they fall spent on the water.**

Trico

Family: Tricorythodidae
Genus: Tricorythodes
Life Cycle: incomplete
Three Life Stages: egg, nymph, adult
    cycle which includes 2 phases: dun
    and spinner
Emergence: July-October
Crawler Mayfly Group

Nymph

Body Description
Eyes: 2 small
Legs: 6
Wings: dark wing pads
Tails: 3
Mobility: incapable of swimming,
    wiggle and undulate to emerge

**Lives in silt, weedy, slower sections of
    streams**

Dun

Body Description
Abdomen: short and stubby
Eyes: 2 small
Legs: 6
Wings: 1 set, smoky transparent, no hind
    wings
Gills: triangular, nearly covering the first
    half of their abdomens
Tails: 2 or 3
Mobility: spends lots of time on surface
    film

Body Color: males are black or chocolate
    colored, (some may be lighter and
    have hint of grey or pale yellow);
    females have olive abdomen and dark
    brown thorax
Size: 3-6mm
Hook Size: 18-22 (18-20 most common)

Spinner

Body Description
Abdomen: short and stubby
Eyes: 2 small
Legs: 6
Wings: 1 set, no hind wings,
    plastic transparent looking
Tails: 3
Body Colors: female, olive abdomen
    and dark brown thorax; male, dark
    brown or black
Mobility: after mating on slow, weedy
    streams, spinner falls are intense,
    blanketing the surface
Size: 3-6mm
Hook Size: 18-22

Western Green Drake

Family: Ephemerelidae
Genus: Drunella
Life Cycle: incomplete
Three Life Stages: egg, nymph, adult
   cycle which includes 2 phases: dun
   and spinner
Emergence: June-July
Crawler Mayflies Group

Nymph

Body Description
Horns: 2
Eyes: large
Abdomen: spurs on last two segments of
   the abdomen
Head: have flat leading edges
Tails: 3
Legs: have stout femurs on all 6
Body Colors: medium-dark browns to
   olive browns
Mobility: strong swimmers and not
   swept away by the water, nymphs in
   faster waters go to calm water before
   emergence, those in medium currents
   stay there and emerge at surface film
Size: 11-15mm, large and somewhat
   stubby

**Found among the rocks and debris in
   medium to fast riffles and runs.**

Dun

Body Description
Wings: 2 sets, large secondary
   wings, dark gray
Tails: 3
Body Colors: bright green & olive
   brown markings, olive & yellow
   trim, color changes soon after
   emergence darkening in as little
   as 1 hour
Mobility: after emergence they stay on
   the water until their wings and tails
   are fully dried and extended; tend to
   have many crippled or damaged duns

Size: 11-15mm
Hook Size: large 10

Spinners

Mating Green Drakes fall soon after dark.
   All three stages are fed upon by trout
   but spinners aren't important foods.

Western March Brown

Family: Heptagenlidae
Genus: Rhithrogena
Life Cycle: incomplete
Three Life Stages: egg, nymph, adult
   cycle which includes 2 phases: dun
   and spinner
Emergence: March-May
Clinger Mayfly Group

Nymph

Body Description
Antennae: 2 short
Head: head is wider than the abdomen
Eyes: large
Gills: large and overlapping under the
   abdomen forming a suction cup to
   help cling and move about the rocks
   in the fast currents
Tails: 3
Legs: 6
Body Color: olive-brown to brown
Mobility: slow swimming and floating;
   they drift long distances before they go
   to the surface
Size: 8-12mm
Hook Size: 10-14

**Live in the faster current of riffles and
   runs in the rocks.**

Dun

Body Description
Antennae: 2 short
Head: flat
Eyes: large

Wings: 2 sets, grayish and highly marked
   with dark brown mottling; distinguish
   from callibaetis because March Browns
   have prominent 2nd wing while
   callibaetis do not
Tails: 2
Legs: 6
Body Color: top is shades of brown;
   bottom is shades of tan
Size: 8-12mm
Hook Size: 10-14

Spinner

Body Description
Wings: clear and heavily
   veined
Body Color: light to medium brown

**After emerging into spinners they mate
   and return to the water to lay their
   eggs but don't normally provide a
   fishable spinner fall.**

Big Yellow May

Family: Ephemeridae
Genus: Hexagenia
Life Cycle: incomplete
Three Life Stages: egg, nymph, adult
   cycle which includes 2 phases: dun
   and spinner
Emergence: May-August
Burrower Mayfly Group

Nymph

Body Description
Antennae: 2, short
Head: tusks on head: rounded projection
   at front of head
Eyes: large
Tails: 3
Wings: pads
Gills: use to circulate throughout their
   burrows
Legs: 6
Body Colors: pale yellow-brown
Mobility: dig U-shaped burrows
Size: 18-35mm
Hook Size: 6-8, 3X Long

**Largest Mayfly. They live in streams
   and lakes where they can have firm
   bottoms to dig burrows.**

Dun

Body Description
Antennae: 2, short
Eyes: 2 large
Tails: 2

Wings: 2 sets, no marks on them but well
   veined
Legs: 6
Body Colors: top, light tan to bright
   yellow with distinct dark markings;
   bottom, unmarked lighter shade of
   top
Mobility: are not fast emergers
Size: 22-35mm
Hook Size: 6-10

Spinner

After spinners emerge they mate high
   above the water. This takes place in
   flight. After this process the male
   falls spent to the water and the female
   returns to lay her eggs, and then falls
   spent to the water. Trout like all stages
   of the Big Yellow May but the spinner
   is least important to the angler.

Brown Drake

Family: Ephemeridae
Genus: Ephemera
Life Cycle: incomplete
Three Life Stages: egg, nymph,
adult cycle which includes 2 phases:
 dun and spinner
Emergence: June-August
Burrower Mayfly Group

Nymph

Body Description
Antennae: 2
Head: has long tusks and u-shaped
    projection from the head
Eyes: large
Legs: 6 strong
Tails: 3
Gills are used to circulate air into their
    shelter
Mobility: quick diggers and good
    swimmers
Body Colors: pale yellow-brown
Size: 12-20mm
Hook Size: 10-12, 3X long

**Nymphs are found in eddies,
    backwaters and moderate currents
    that have fine silt, sand and gravel
    bottoms.**

Dun

Body Description
Antennae: 2
Eyes: large
Legs: 6

Tails: 3
Wings: 2 sets, mottled grey, dark marks
    on wings
Body Colors: yellow-brown including
    dark markings on top of abdomen
Size: 15-20mm
Hook Size: 8-12

Spinner

Body Description
The dun emerges into a spinner and
    flies into the stream's foliage banks.
    Mating flights transpire and the female
    returns to the water to lay eggs. There
    aren't enough spinners to produce a
    good spinner fall.

**Brown Drakes are mistaken for Green
    Drakes. They are the same size and
    distinguished by heavily patterned
    wings with mottling in both the dun
    & spinner.**

Blue-Winged Olive

Family: Baetidae
Genus: Baetis
Life Cycle: incomplete
Three Life Stages: egg, nymph, adult
    cycle which includes 2 phases: dun
    and spinner
Emergence: Fall and Spring
Swimmer Mayfly Group

Nymph

Body Description

Antennae: two antennae on top of head
Abdomen: 10 segments
Wings: one visible pair of wing pads on
    top of thorax
Gills: top and sides of abdomen
Tails: 3
Legs: 6 with one sharp claw on each
Body Colors: olive to dark brown
Mobility: quick and agile
Size: 3-12mm
Hook Size: 14-20 2X long

**Blue wing olive mayflies may appear
    anywhere in a stream but are best
    found in riffles and weedy runs.**

Dun

Body Description

Antennae: 2
Abdomen: 10 segments
Wings: 2 sets drab colored
Tails: 2
Legs: 6

Body Colors: olive, or variations of olive
    brown or gray, pale light green
Mobility: fly to streambed foliage
Size: 3-9mm
Hook Size: 14-22

Spinner

Body Description

Antennae:
Abdomen: 10 segments
Wings: 2 sets —clear, hind wings
    are difficult to see; they are small,
    long and narrow
Legs: 6
Body Colors: females, olive-brown
    dark reddish brown; males, same,
    but part of the abdomen translucent
Size: 3-12mm
Hook Size: 14-22

**After mating the female lays eggs on
    the water's surface or sometimes
    will crawl under the surface and lay
    them on submerged objects.**

Flavs (Small Green Drakes, or Flavilineas)

Family: Ephemerellidae
Genus: Drunella
Life Cycle: incomplete
Three Life Stages: egg, nymph, adult cycle
    which includes 2 phases: dun and spinner
Emergence: June-August
Crawler Mayfly Group

Nymphs

Body Description
Antennae: 2
Wings: pads
Legs: 6, stout front legs have teeth on
    front edge
Abdomen: no long spines
Eyes: large
Tails: 3
Body Colors: browns with olive tones
Mobility: become more active before
    emergence
Size: 7-9mm
Hook Size: 12-16

Found among rocks in faster current flows. They emerge from slower water by faster flows and from runs with slow to medium currents.

Dun

Body Description
Antennae: 2
Wings: 2 sets, hind wings have
    pointed edges, dark grey
Legs: 6

Eyes: large
Tails: 3
Body Colors: light olive with yellow tones
Mobility: must wait on the water floating
    or drifting after emergence for their
    wings to unfold before flying
Size: 7-9mm
Hook Size: 14-16

Spinner

Body Description
Antennae: 2
Wings: 2 sets, hind wings
    have pointed edges
Legs: 6
Eyes: large
Tails: 3
Body Colors: dark olive to olive brown
Size: 7-9mm
Hook Size: 14-16

One day after emergence they are sexually mature. Male & females meet in swarms; after mating males fall spent on the water or ground, females hover close to the water, deposit their eggs then fall spent.

Gray Drake
Family: Siphlonuridae
Genus: Siphlonurus
Life Cycle: incomplete
Three Life Stages: egg, nymph, adult
   cycle which includes 2 phases: dun
   and spinner
Emergence: April-October
Swimmer Mayfly Group

Nymph

Body Description
Antennae: 2, short
Abdomen: double-flapped gills on first
   segments
Eyes: large
Tails: 3
Wings: pads
Legs: 6
Mobility: hair fringed tails make them
   rapid swimmers

**Most dense populations are found in
   slow-moving streams. They can be
   found among the grass and roots of
   undercut banks. Diet includes plant
   matter, smaller insects but mostly
   midge larvae. Trout can get fat
   feasting on these nymphs.**

Dun

Duns are not discussed because they are
   not common for trout consumption.

Spinner

Body Description
Antennae: 2, short
Eyes: large
Tails: 2
Wings: 2 pair that are transparent (no
   mottling distinguishes them from
   brown drakes)
Legs: 6

**After mating the males often fall spent
   on the ground or water with the
   female returning to the water to
   lay her eggs. When her task is
   completed the female falls spent to
   the water. The spinner falls can be
   very heavy where the population is
   large in springs.**

Speckle-Wing Quill

Family: Baetidae
Genus: Callibaetis
Life Cycle: incomplete
Three Life Stages: egg, nymph, adult
    cycle which includes 2 phases: dun
    and spinner
Emergence: April-October
Swimmer Mayfly Group

Nymph

Body Description

Antennae: two long antennae
Abdomen: 10 segments
Wings: wing pads
Gills: top and sides of abdomen
Tails: three of equal length
Legs: 6 with one sharp claw on each
Body Colors: mottled brown-tannish
    olive
Mobility: very agile, crawl about weed
    beds in short bursts of speed when
    hatching
Size: 6-12mm
Hook Size: 12-16

**Found in still and slow-moving weedy
waters.**

Dun

Body Description

Wings: 2 sets, highly mottled wings are
    semi-transparent, small hind wings
Tails: 2
Legs: 6

Body Colors: top is brownish olive to
    gray; bottom, light tan to olive
Mobility: after emergence quickly flies off
    to streamside foliage
Size: 6-12mm
Hook Size: 12-18

Spinner

Body Description

Wings: 2 sets including small hind wings
    (plastic like), clear, less mottled than
    dun
Eyes: small
Tails: 2
Legs: 6
Body Colors: top, gray or brown; bottom,
    light shade of top color
Size: 6-12mm
Hook size: 12-18 (14-16 most Common)

**Males die shortly after mating, females
wait for about 5 days before laying
eggs, then die.**

Caddisflies

Order: Trichoptera
Number of species: over 1200
Life Cycle: complete metamorphosis
Four Life Stages: egg, larva, pupa, adult

Larva

Body Description

Abdomen: 9 segments
Thorax: 3 segments
Legs: 6
Worm-like appearance, fragile
Size: 6-22, up to 1 1/2" in length
Most are case builders (case made of
    bottom debris which protects fragile
    larvae)
Activity: some are free roaming but move
    at a slow crawl

Pupa

Body Description

Wings: Distinguished by folding wings in
    a downward position under the body's
    sides
Activity: may capture an air bubble to
    float to the surface

Adult

Body Description

Antenna: long (2x body)
Wings: tent like wings fold over body
Tails: none
Colors: mottled shades: olives, browns,
    tans, grays, yellows
Activity: fast & erratic
Hook Size: 6-22, 14-16 most common

**There are five groups of caddisflies
    which are determined by the larva's
    behavior: free-living caddis, saddle-
    case caddis, net-spinning caddis,
    tube-case caddis, and purse-case
    caddis.**

**Caddisflies are typically found in cold,
    oxygen-rich water such as mountain
    streams where there are riffles and
    runs.**

Midges

Order: Diptera (2 winged insects)
Family: Chironomidae
Over 175 genera and 1000 species
Life Cycle: complete
Four Stage Metamorphosis: egg, larva, pupa, and adult
(Midges sit with their forelegs raised up in the air.
   Mosquitoes sit with their hind legs in the air.)

Larva

Body Description

The body is wormlike having 3 segments to the thorax, 9 for the abdominal segments with no distinctive gills, visible legs or wing pads with proleg and head. (Mosquitoes have 10 segments) Large eyes are also located on the head. They generally inhabit the bottom of the area they live in and have sinuous undulations or crawling movements. Their body colors are a wide variety of black, grey, olive, yellow, white, cream, ruby, amber, purple, olive green, brown and some contain hemoglobin. They range in size from approximately 1/16-1".

Pupa

Body Description

The midge pupa is distinguished by an enlarged head that appears to be fused as one with the thorax. There are plume like gills on top of the head that look like antennae and also on the tip of the abdomen. Under the top of the thorax are enlargements that hold the folded wings and legs. The segmented abdomen is much smaller than the thorax in diameter. The pupa is free swimming but slow and is a bottom dweller.

Adult

Body Description

The adult has 6 very long slender legs that are 2 to 2 ½ times longer than the entire body and make a round star-like silhouette. When at rest the one pair of wings is flat and lies at a slight angle to the body and can measure up to 1". The antennae are plume like and are especially large on the male. There is not a tail and the abdomen is segmented. The thorax and the head are extra large. Body colors are assorted, anywhere from dark blacks, greens, tans, with light striped abdomen. A few hours after mating both sexes die but don't necessarily fall to the water like the mayflies and therefore are not a significant source of food for trout.

Mosquito

Order: Diptera (2 winged insects)

Life Cycle: complete

Four Stage Metamorphosis: egg, larva, pupa, and adult

Mosquitoes sit with their hind legs in the air. (Midges sit with their forelegs raised up in the air.)

Larva

Body Description

Larva is similar to the midge larva except they have 10 segments instead of 9.

Pupa

Body Description

Mosquito pupa is similar to the midge except they have a respiratory tube and have a 2-3 day life span at the surface film.

Adult

Body Description

Adult mosquitoes are like the midge except the female has a needle to bite. Their body colors are: black white, and tan white.

Female

Male

Craneflies

Order: Diptera (2 winged insects)

Life Cycle: complete

Four Stage Metamorphosis: egg, larva, pupa, and adult

Craneflies are very large Diptera which resemble large mosquitoes but are preferred by fish because of their abundance. The pupa is not available for fish. The cranefly larva is one to two inches thick and meaty, burrowing in and around the bottom structures of lakes and streams. When the larva is dislodged they curl up into a ball or react by elongating like leeches. No matter what stage the larva is in, trout will eat them. Cranefly adults actively mate, laying eggs along the water's edge. They dance and flutter, catching the trout's attention, making craneflies readily available to them.

Damselflies

Order: Odonata
Suborder: Zygoptera
Life Cycle: incomplete
Three Life Stages: egg, nymph, and adult
Life Span: anywhere from 2-4 years

Nymph

Body Description

Antennae: none
Eyes: very large, compound on small head, as wide or wider than thorax
Wings: 2 pair pads
Thorax: short and larger
Gills: 3 large distinctive paddlelike tails that are actually gills
Abdomen: long and slender, no gills, plumes or other projections on thorax or abdomen
Mouth: appendages tucked under the head
Legs: 6 long
Body Colors: olives and browns, lighter body
Mobility: side to side wiggling motion like a tadpole
Size: 1-1 ½"

Adult

Body Description

Antennae: none visible
Eyes: large, on top of head, eyes are spaced the size of an eye
Tail: none
Wings: 2 pairs, equal in size. Each has a distinctive narrow yolk or stalk at base of thorax. When at rest they are folded over and appear to be one
Abdomen: long and slender, segmented
Legs: short and crowded, weak
Body Colors: olives, greens, blues and black
Mobility: very graceful, extremely fast fliers

Dragonflies

Order: Odonata
Suborder: Anisoptera
Life Cycle: incomplete
Three Life Stages: egg, nymph, and adult
Life Span: anywhere from 2-4 years

Weed dweller   Mud dweller

Nymph

Body Description

Antennae: 2 very small

Eyes: 2 very large compound eyes that almost touch each other and make the head look small

Mouth: (lower lip) able to reach out to grasp or seize prey, under the thorax and head

Tail: none

Wings: pads

Gills: no outer surface

Legs: 6, spider like and tightly based

Abdomen: very wide, thick and compressed

Body Colors: camouflage to environment, mottled browns, olive & brownish black, shades of yellow

Mobility: very active. They crawl, dart, and free swim and hunt for food

Adult

Body Description

Antennae: 2 very small

Eyes: 2 very large compound eyes that touch or almost touch each other on top of the head, very dominant

Wings: 2 sets, hind wings are wider than forewings, strongly veined glassy wings of equal length. They separate horizontally at rest or in flight, can spread up to 6"

Legs: very small held tightly to the thorax

Abdomen: long, slender and segmented

Tail: none

Body Colors: incredible metallic fluorescent shades. Colors vary from bright greens, purples, and clarets, rusty reds, burnt oranges, blues and blacks

Golden Stonefly

Family: Perlidae
Genus: Hesperoperla or Calineuria
Life Cycle: incomplete
Three Life Stages: egg, nymph and adult
Emergence: May-August

Nymph

Body Description
Antennae: 2 long
Eyes: 2 fair sized
Tails: 2
Wings: pads
Gills: tufts on bottom of each leg
Legs: 6 with claws on each
Abdomen: 10 segments
Body Colors: medium light tan with pale
    golden yellow segments – predominate
    on belly
Mobility: poor swimmers, must drift
    along the currents until they can settle
    on the bottom
Size: up to 1 inch, 22-38 mm
Hook Size: 6-8, 3X long

**Depending on water temperature
    and food accessibility, they spend
    anywhere from 2-3 years in the
    nymphal stage.**

Adult

Body Description
Antennae: 2 long
Eyes: 2 beady
Tails: 2
Wings: highly veined
Gills: remnants of tufts left on legs
Legs: 6 with claws on each
Abdomen: 10 segments
Body Colors: light tan body with
    segmentation of yellowish-gold, belly
    more predominately yellowish-gold
Size: up to 1 ½"–smaller than Giant
    Salmonflies
Hook Size: 6-8, 3X long

Mating occurs in same locations as
    emergence. 1-2 days after emergence
    the adults lay their eggs by returning
    to the water and contacting the surface
    several times briefly during the day.

**The Brownstone Stonefly is similar
    to the Golden Stonefly but its
    coloration is somewhat darker with
    tan/cream replacing the gold.**

Giant Salmonfly (Stonefly)

Order: Plecoptera
Family: Pteronarcidae
Genus: Pteronarcys
Life Cycle: incomplete
Three Life Stages: egg, nymph and adult
Emergence: April-July

Nymph

Body Description
Antennae: 2 long
Eyes: 2 fair sized
Tails: 2
Wings: pads on top of thorax
Gills: tufts are under the front part of the
    body or may be absent
Abdomen: 10 segments-evenly cylindrical
Legs: 6 with sharp claws on each
Mobility: poor swimmers
Body Colors: dark brown to black
Size: 1 ½" or more, 25-50 mm
Hook Size: 4-8, 3X long

Nymphs take anywhere from 2-4 years to emerge depending on the temperature and abundance of food. They cling to the undersides of rocks where they feed on plant debris.

Adult

Body Description
Antennae: 2 long
Eyes: 2 fair sized
Tails: 2
Wings: 2 pairs–highly veined
Abdomen: 10 segments
Legs: 6 with claws on each
Mobility: clumsy fliers (females)
Size: up to 2 ½", 30-50 mm
Hook Size: 4-8, 3X long

Females return several times to the water to deposit eggs. They will live anywhere from a few days to 1 week after depositing their eggs.

Little Yellow Salleys

Order: Plecoptera
Family: Perlodidae
Genus: Isoperta
Life Cycle: incomplete
Three Life Stages: egg, nymph and adult
Emergence: July-September

Nymph

Body Description
Antennae: 2 long
Eyes: 2 black beady
Tails: 2
Legs: 6
Abdomen: 10 segments
Mobility: active predators that crawl among the rocks looking for insects
Body Color: transparent golden yellow to dark brown with ribbing
Size: 3/8"-5/8", 7-16 mm
Hook Size: 8-14, 2X long

Stonefly nymphs are best found in cold water streams with the biggest population living in fast flowing streams in the mountains.

Adult

Body Description
Antennae: 2 long
Eyes: 2 black beady
Tails: 2
Legs: 6
Abdomen: 10 segments
Mobility: very active, often seen flying out over the water and around the foliage
Body Color: pale to a bright yellow translucent color
Size: ½"-3/4", 7-16 mm
Hook Size: 10-16

Females glide, fly or drop over riffles and runs to deposit their eggs. This may take several times before all the eggs are deposited. Many females end up on the water.

Water Boatman

Adult

Body Description
Water boatmen are shaped like a flat
football and average in length from
1/3"-1/2" maximum. Their oar
shaped legs are distinguishing because
of their oaring locomotion. Boatmen
carry a bubble on their belly. Their
body color is a drab brownish black
with subtle barring of dirty yellow,
brown olive, gray-brown. The belly is
a light to dark brown or dirty white to
dull yellow.

Snails

Adult

Body Description
Snails have a rather unique shell with a
retractable body. Their body colors
usually match the colorization of the
water bottom, with olives, browns, or
blackish shells.

Leeches, Eels, & Lampreys

Leeches

Leeches are used best for catching large trout while flyfishing. These parasites live on reptiles, snails or cold-blooded fish; some live off plants and dead animals. They don't have eyes but have a high sense of smell and touch. Their highly developed muscular system and multi-segmented body allows them to change their body form from short and fat to thin and elongated. Both ends of the leech have strong suction cups to hold on to the host or bottom structures. They can reach anywhere from 1"- 6" in length. Leeches have a wide range of color, anywhere from light crème to black, brown, gray, or olive, with lateral stripes. They may have mottled spots or markings.

Eels

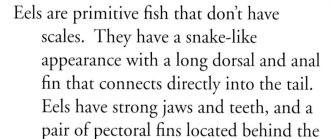

Eels are primitive fish that don't have scales. They have a snake-like appearance with a long dorsal and anal fin that connects directly into the tail. Eels have strong jaws and teeth, and a pair of pectoral fins located behind the gill openings. This primitive fish is a scavenger as well as a predator of other fish species. Eels are unusual because they spawn in salt water but live in fresh water with some still staying behind and living in salt water. They are swift, strong swimmers and prefer to live on the bottoms of lakes and streams.

Lampreys

Lampreys are blood sucking parasites that are primitive fish with cartilage skeletons and no scales. They have a round, sucking, disk mouth and a long, double, dorsal fin which attaches exactly with their tails. Just behind their heads they have a series of horizontal gill holes. Their wormlike larvae can be found in freshwater streams buried in the mud or sand bottoms. After emergence, these parasites are free swimming and are eaten by trout only until they are about 2"-8" long. Lampreys mostly attack fish as parasites. They live close to bottom structures. Their coloration varies from silvery to dirty olive or brown with a lighter side.

Other Fish Foods

Sculpins

These fish are loners and like to hug the bottoms of streams and lakes. They usually feed on insects, snails, aquatic worms, other fish and crustaceans. Like trout they want to inhabit lakes and streams that give them the best oxygen, food, cover and suitable temperature. Sculpins average one inch to six or eight inches in length. A top view of the fish shows pronounced tear drop, wedge-shaped, and wide-flaring pectoral fins. Their shape is similar to a bullhead with a wide head which tapers towards the tail. Large trout don't even need to leave the bottom when sculpins are around because they are such poor swimmers and don't generally flee up or to the shallows when chased. Colors are a lighter belly, dirty cream, tan or olive.

Baitfish Minnows

Minnows, sometimes referred to as shiners are an important forage fish for larger prey. They are in the same group as dace, whitefish, chubs, perch, fall fish, and sticklebacks. Since there are multiple life cycles, there are plenty of them to choose from anywhere from ½" to 6" or longer. These fish feed on aquatic and terrestrial insects, small fish or may even be vegetarians. When chased by a predator they are excellent swimmers maneuvering to escape, hiding below structures or darting to the surface. They have a golden olive coloration.

Threadfin Shad

The threadfin shad are fish that are usually in open waters and run in close-schooling, fast-swimming groups. These schools appear to be silvery black clouds. They can be found in waters that are warmer than 45°. They grow up to 3 inches and in some 2 year olds may be as large as 4"-7". They are characterized by a dark eyelike marking with a thick shaped belly. They have silver sides with a darker back. Alewives and smelts are also from this group of fish.

Crustaceans

Scientific Name: Amphipoda
(2 types of legs)

Scuds

There are over 50 different species of the scud. This fascinating crustacean looks and acts like saltwater shrimp so they are often called freshwater shrimp. Scuds have been successfully introduced into man-made tail waters, lakes and reservoirs. There is a wide variety of colors even among the same species, same generation and area. Males are smaller than the females and their diet and growth rate will vary. Scuds have two long antennae on top of the head that curve forward and down. On the six abdominal segments there are 6 pairs of appendages with 7 thoracic segments. The first thoracic segment and the head are fused together. There are 7 pairs of legs with the first 2 pairs being club-like claws. Scuds resemble an armadillo when they die because of the C-shaped fetal position they form. Their body colors are different grays, browns, olives, tans, creams, some bright green, opalescent blue, red and some transparent colors.

Sow Bugs: Isopoda

Common names for sow bugs are cress bugs and pill bugs. They are closely related to scuds and have the same life cycle as the scud. Other relatives are terrestrial potato bugs. Sow bugs have 8 very distinct flat segments, 2 pairs of antennae–one small and one large. On the rear segment there are two paddle-like flat tails. The underside of the body is white. These bugs are very slow crawlers and will helplessly drift in the current and may roll up in a pill shape. They are nocturnal and can be active in very cold water. Cold water conditions in the off seasons (fall, winter and spring) are excellent for fishing.

Crayfish: Decapods

Crayfish are an important source of fish
food because of their large size and
nutritional content. Characteristics of
the crayfish are: five strong pairs of
legs with the first three pairs having
clawed ends, with the first set of legs
much larger with strong pincher
claws that are like a crab; two beady
eyes; a flap-like paddle at the end
of a segmented tail; and two pair of
antennae. When the crayfish sheds
its exoskeleton and becomes a soft
shelled creature it is most vulnerable
to trout. They have good mobility,
either crawling in a forward or reverse
movement or tail swimming in a fast
darting motion. As nocturnal bottom
dwellers, they live under shallow
streamside or lakeside structures,
close to rocks, logs, weed beds, moss
beds, old cans, and tree bark and they
dig dens. They are both scavengers
and predators. Crayfish prefer warm
temperatures (55°-65°F) and are
dormant in colder temperatures below
42°F.

Aquatic Insect Collection

The following equipment is helpful in catching insects. The green net can recover flying insects and the gray net placed in the stream collects drifting insects. The stomach pump can recover ingested insects from living fish. The 35 mm film canister stores the samples.

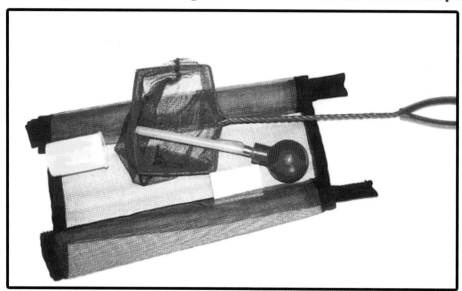

Matching The Hatch

After collecting an aquatic food I go through my fly box and try to match it. Here are a few examples of succesful matches.

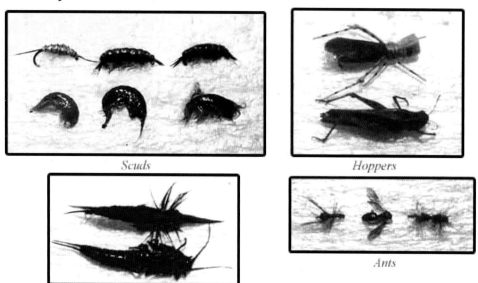

Scuds

Hoppers

Stoneflies

Ants

Matches (continued)

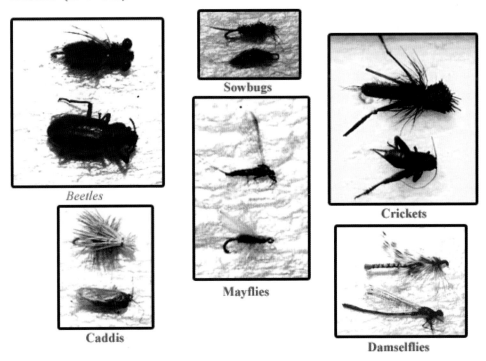

Beetles

Sowbugs

Mayflies

Crickets

Caddis

Damselflies

Matches (continued)

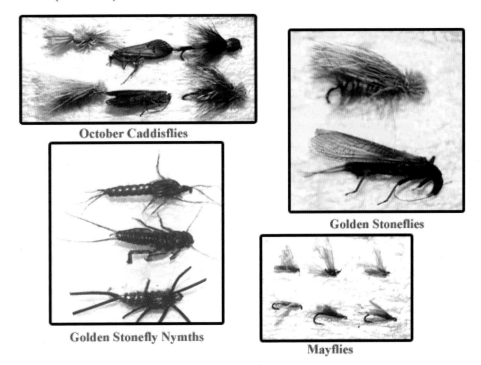

October Caddisflies

Golden Stoneflies

Golden Stonefly Nymths

Mayflies

Matches (continued)

Blue Wing Olive Mayflies

Caddisflies

Small stoneflies

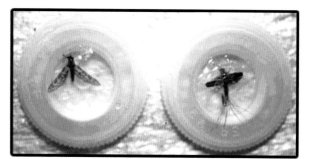
Callibaetis Mayflies

Matches (continued)

Cased Caddisfles

Wasps

Snails

Leeches

APPROACH 4

The goal of the approach is to place an angler [you] into the best position to present the fly without alarming the fish. The following variables influence your approach: the fish's position, water clarity, light intensity, hatch intensity, current speed, wind direction, cover placement, casting obstructions, current maladies, and sound vibrations. After examining these factors, the angler's choice of position is made; next, the actual approach takes place.

Fish's Postion

In moving water, fish face upstream. Before planning an approach take into account the fish's location in terms of its exact position and depth. Its depth determines the window size through which a fish views the outside world. A fish holding close to the surface has a much smaller window to see through than a deeply holding fish.

Approaching a shallow fish is easier than a deep one. The smaller the window, the less likely a fish can see you. Try hiding from the fish by staying outside of its vision window.

Fish are overly cautious to vibrations sensed by their lateral lines. However, shallow-holding fish may be more alert because they are more vulnerable to predators and will streak for cover at the slightest provocation.

Water Clarity

Clear water improves the fish's vision; stained water obscures its vision. In addition, fish are more alert in clear water as compared to stained water. Most predators use their eye sight to find fish. An osprey must first see a fish before it can catch one. A cloak of stained water simplifies the approach, while clear water complicates the approach.

Light Intensity

Light intensity plays a vital role. With increased light the fish's vision improves, and they will become more wary of predators. The sun's angle determines the amount of light entering the water. Low light angles penetrate the surface less because more of it is subject to refraction. That's why it is easier to approach fish at dawn and dusk rather than at midday. Consequently, it is easier to approach fish during the seasons with lowered sunlight angles (winter, spring and fall).

Likewise, it is more difficult to approach fish during the summer season. The high sunlight angle illuminates the water and improves the fish's vision. As a result, the more light that is present, the more observant the fish will become.

A bright sun over your back may conceal your position from the fish because the glare makes it difficult to detect your presence. You are hidden by the sun's brightness. But if you cast a sudden shadow over the fish, you may alarm them because they fear that this shadow might be a bird swooping down upon them.

Hatch Variables

During heavy hatches the fish may hold just below the surface which restricts their vision window. When hatches are sparse fish hold deeper so that they can view a wider area looking for insects and deeper holding fish may see you better. Fish can become less cautious during heavy hatches because they are preoccupied feeding. The longer a hatch persists the less wary the fish becomes. It can be easier to closely approach fish late in a heavy hatch than earlier in the same hatch.

Current Speed

Current speed influences the vertical position that a fish can hold. The faster the current the less likely a fish can hold close to the surface. It must seek a place resting in the slower deeper currents; consequently, its

vision window is enlarged. The slower the current the shallower a fish can hold, and its vision window is diminished. But the faster currents have a more broken surface that obscures the fish's vision; therefore, its outside world is more distorted in faster flows. Slower currents have calmer surfaces which are easier for the fish to see through.

Wind

Breezes cause the surface to be broken up, and this impairs the fish's vision. Calmer water presents the fish with a clearer vision field. Additionally birds of prey have difficulty spotting fish under a broken surface. Fish are easier to approach  on a windy day as compared to a calm one. Also, the wind moves the riparian growth and fish have trouble spotting your movements.

Cover

Bank side and aquatic cover can impair the fish's vision; consequently, use bank side brush to conceal you during your approach, and to hide your position. Because light refraction can sometimes allow fish to see around corners, fish may be able to see you when you cannot see them. (See Diagram 1)

By taking the fish's vision window into account you can mask your approach by placing cover between you and the fish. But watch out for the light refraction phenomenon that permits fish to see around corners.

Casting Obstructions

Design your approach so that your final position is not complicated by casting obstructions. Bank side cover may impair your casting stroke making it difficult to make a presentation. It is best to avoid false casting over a fish, and roll casting often bothers the surface too much to be useful.

With planning, your approach can place you in a position relatively free of casting obstructions.

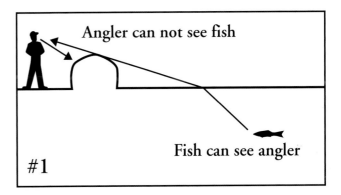

Angler can not see fish

Fish can see angler

#1

Current Maladies

Current eddies and seams can perplex your presentation by causing undue drag. Whirlpools and conflicting currents play havoc on your fly's drift. Usually your presentations goal is a natural drag-free drift; furthermore, the need for excessive line mending may alarm fish. Select a position that best simplifies your presentation.

Sound Vibrations

Fish have a special sensory organ located in their lateral line. With this organ fish can detect underwater sounds and disturbances. This lateral line is so sensitive it can detect a fish's prey. An injured minnow's struggle is readily perceived. Sound and other vibrations carry better underwater; therefore, be cautious to eliminate vibrations that may be detected by the fish. Heavy footsteps while walking or wading are to be avoided. Careless wading can cause the gravel to strike each other alarming the fish. Boat noises are to be avoided. An aluminum boat can sound like a bass drum. Carpet the boat's floors and storage areas to dampen the noise. Talking is poorly transmitted underwater,

although very loud noises can be conveyed. So go ahead and talk but don't vibrate the water. The basic rule is to avoid all motions which cause underwater vibrations.

In summary, after judging each of these variables, plan your approach carefully. Sometimes so many of these variables are stacked on the fish's side that a successful approach may be just too complex. It would be better to find another fish. When these variables are stacked in your favor, the approach may be as simple as walking or wading directly to the spot that you want to fish. Remember that the approach plan should be to remain out of the fish's vision and hearing. Move stealthily like a blue heron. Herons are professional fish stalkers, and much can be learned by observing their methods. Make motions slowly and deliberately and try to blend in with the environment. Dress accordingly with colors and patterns that intermix with the background. Once in position, stop and rest the fish; subsequently, the fish may accept the angler as part of the landscape. Make your first presentation your best one.

5
PRESENTATIONS

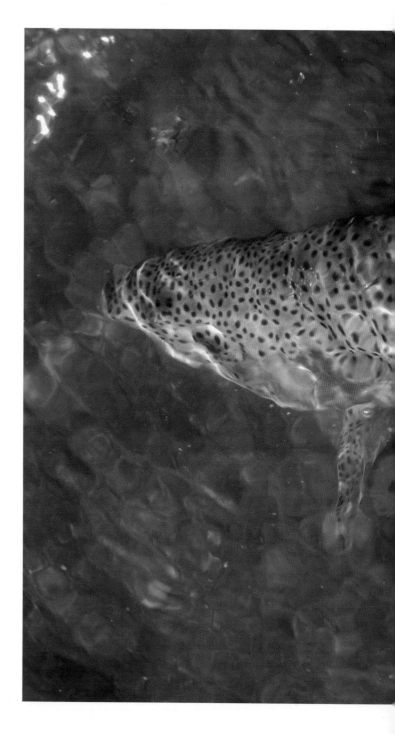

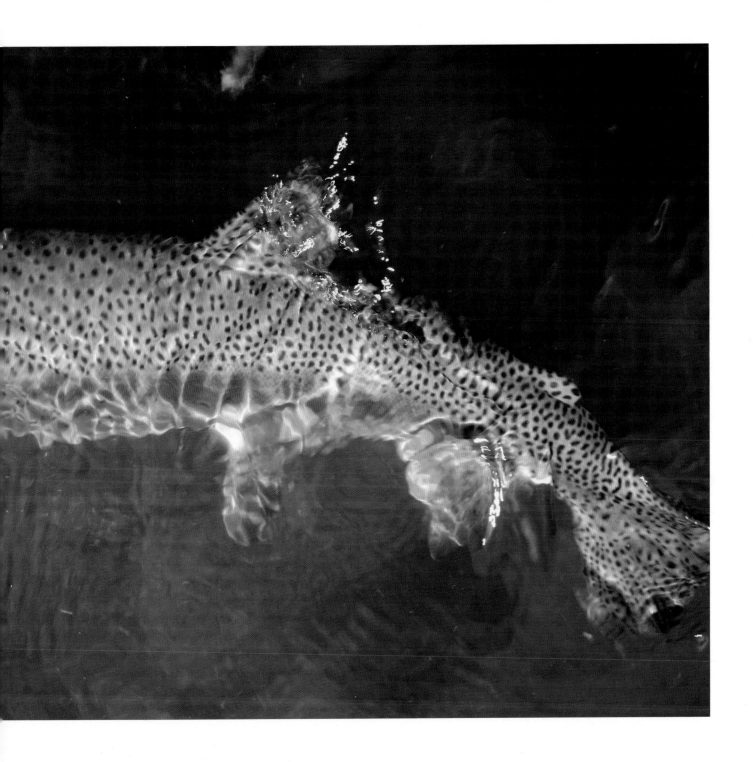

Dry Fly Natural Drift

The natural drift's purpose is to provide a drag-free drift of the fly. During hatching and egg-laying activities, mayflies are motionless creatures. They are mimicked well by this method. Drifting along the surface, mayflies are at the mercy of the current. To drift unnaturally is termed drag, and it's caused by the leader pulling on the fly. Drag pulls the fly across the current in an unnatural motion. Effective presentations are drag free.

The following is a list of methods designed to present a fly in a natural, drag-free manner; they are used to imitate placid insects.

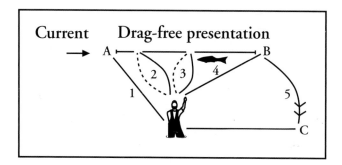

Classic 3/4 Upstream

1. Cast is made 3/4 upstream by a straight cast or a reach cast.
2. Mends are appropriately made to extend the drift so that the line/leader does not float at a different rate than the fly.
   A. Upstream mending generally slows the fly's drift.
   B. Downstream mending generally speeds the fly's drift.
3. Ideal target position is directly or slightly downstream from the angler's position.
4. Line is released to extend float to the 3/4 downstream position.
5. Fly is fished under tension as it swings in an arc directly downstream from the angler.
6. Fly/line/leader is picked up and recast.

Young's Presentation

A. Reach cast is made 3/4 upstream.
   1. Cast is made deliberately too long.
B. Raise the rod upward to pull the fly into lane.
   1. Once fly is in position, drop the rod downward. This allows slack line to extend the float across the desired feeding lane.
   2. When raising the rod upwards, do so in an upstream motion because this mends the line for a longer, drag-free float.
C. Mend line to prolong the drift.
   1. Upstream mends generally slow the fly's drift.
   2. Downstream mends generally speed the fly's drift.
D. Raise rod upwards to reposition the fly into Lane 2.
   1. Repeat B1, B2 and C.
E. Fish fly under tension as it swings downstream to E.
F. Pick up and recast.

Note: As rod is pulled upwards it is also extended upstream to reposition the line belly upstream. (This acts like a reach cast by precisely repositioning the fly and mending the line upstream.)

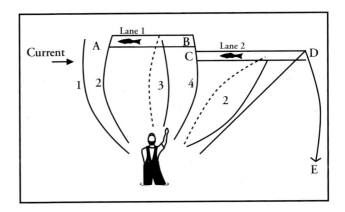

Advantages of Young's Presentation

1. It is an easy presentation to accurately position the fly into the desired feeding lane.
2. It allows the angler to fish multiple feeding lanes in a single cast.
3. It readily provides a long drag free drift precisely where you want it.
4. It is an exceptional method for sight fishing to rising fish.
5. An accurate cast is not needed. Only a cast made too far is used.

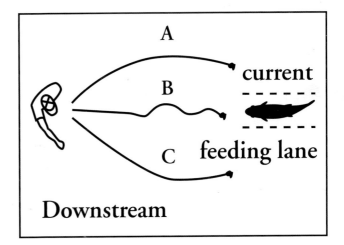

Downstream

The downstream presentation is useful for calm spring creek and tail water streams. The fly is presented to the fish first without any disturbances from the leader or line. When the casting planes are made away from the fish's location, the fish are undisturbed by overhead false casting and line spray. Many times fish are wary of overhead motions which may simulate birds of prey. Additionally, the downstream presentation is simple and effective; perhaps its only disadvantage is that the fly needs to be accurately cast.

Downstream Method

A. Make a reach cast slightly upstream with the fly accurately landing in the feeding lane. Next, lower the rod tip horizontally to the surface; track the fly downstream by reaching with the rod pointed directly towards the fly.

B. Allow the fly to drift well past the fish's position and then make the line swing away by moving away from the feeding lane. Pick up the line for another cast.

Other Useful Downstream Presentations

There are various other methods of presenting a fly downstream. Simply feeding out slack line is one of them. An up-and-down rod shaking or a side-by-side wiggling motion can play out additional line; also, a wiggle cast made directly downstream extends the fly's drift as the line uncoils. Both the slide and the mini-slide methods afford additional downstream presentations.

Again, the advantages of a downstream presentation are: the fish sees the fly first without any disturbances by the line and leader; the line/leader is never false cast over the fish, and a natural dead drift is created.

Both of the above methods present the fly downstream by playing out slack line in a serpentine manner. When the line straightens the dead drift is over.

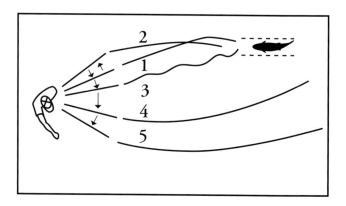

Slide Method

1. Use a downstream cast directed purposefully distant to the feeding lane.

2. Reposition flies straight into the feeding lane so that the fly is about 3-5 feet upstream of the fish's position. This is done by extending the rod to position No. 2, then watching the line/leader/fly move to the targeted area.

3. Quickly lower rod to the No. 3 position to allow slack line and a drag-free drift.

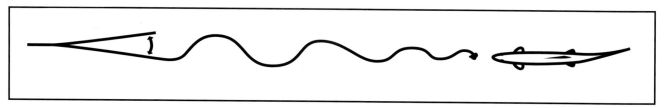

4. If fish refuses the fly, move the rod to position No. 4; allow the fly and line to swing well past the feeding lane.

5. Extend the rod to position No. 5; pause it to straighten the line; next recast the fly.

Advantages:

1. This is an easy method to place the fly precisely to a targeted fish.
2. The fly is delivered first ahead of the leader and line.
3. False casting over the fish is eliminated.

Disadvantage:

The straightened leader is vulnerable to mini-turbulences which may cause unnoticed drag. Employing a long, flexible tippet helps correct this fault.

Mini-Slide Method

The mini-slide presentation offers the fly to 2 or 3 fish in different feeding lanes with the same cast. The fish must be progressively farther away from you in a downstream order.

1. The rod is raised and repositioned to fish #2.
2. The rod is lowered and line is fed out allowing the drag-free drift.

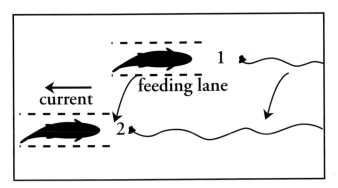

Advantages:

1. With a single cast the angler can present the fly to several different fish.
2. This method reduces the number of casts which minimizes alarming wary fish.
3. With ease the angler can cast to pods of feeding fish.

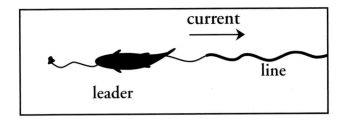

Upstream Presentation

The upstream presentation places the leader directly over the fish's back and the fly lands directly in front of the fish. Try to cast precisely between the fish's eyes. Fish see poorly directly above their backs and a fly gently delivered on a flexible tippet may go unnoticed. This presentation can be a deadly method demanding extreme casting accuracy and delivery. Using an open looped delivery cast helps slow down the fly and line speed which prevents water splashes from the line. However, this method is limited to shorter casts.

The distance to lead a fish depends upon the depth that the fish is holding. Since a fish's vision window expands the deeper it holds, a deep holding fish must be led farther than a shallower holding fish. This allows the fly to land just outside of its vision window. Use caution to make sure that the line and leader junction lands well in back of the fish.

Also a deeper holding fish takes longer to rise than a shallower holding fish. Simply, the deeper fish has a greater distance to travel than a shallow fish.

7/8 Upstream Delivery

The 7/8 upstream delivery presents the fly without placing the line over the fish. The cast is made at about a 1:00 o'clock position with 12:00 o'clock directly upstream from the angler. Only a small tippet segment travels over the feeding lane. This presentation easily furnishes a drag free float.

However, this 7/8 presentation has two disadvantages. First, the false casting over the fish's position may

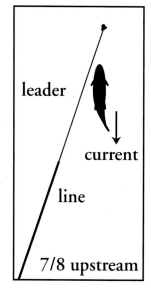

leader

current

line

7/8 upstream

alarm a wary fish. Second, the cast must be accurately made to land precisely into the feeding lane. Fine, flexible tippets and delicate casting help overcome these disadvantages. A rippled surface helps disguise this delivery.

Cast precisely to a targeted area about six feet upstream from the fish. Retrieve the slack line as it drifts back downstream.

Line Mending

Line mending is a repositioning of the line on the water so that its new position extends the fly's drift. Plainly, mends are upstream (upwind) or downstream rod flips which reposition the line belly while it is adrift.

Mending is essential to many presentations; both dry and wet fly methods call for line mending. A simple flip of the wrist mends the line. Upstream flips tend to slow down the fly's drift; likewise, downstream flips hasten the fly's drift.

A stream's diverse current speed causes the need for mending and determines the direction of the mend. For example, when the fly is in faster current than its line, a downstream mend extends the fly's drift. On the other hand, when the fly is in a slower current than its line an upstream mend extends the fly's drift. Since streams seldom have a uniform current, the angler is constantly confronted with mixed current speeds. Common sense determines the direction the line is mended.

An upstream mend repositions the line belly to float at the same position as the fly; hence mending lengthens the fly's drift by preventing drag.

As you fish out a cast, constantly watch the fly and line position. As the fish's relationship to the line changes, correct the line by mending it in the appropriate direction. Optimally, the mending goal is to keep the line, leader, and fly in a straight line. Mending retains this straight alignment.

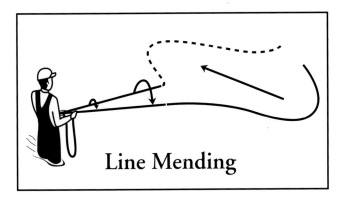

Line Mending

Wrist Roll Mend

As the wrist roll starts, the rod angle is about 0 degrees and arches to a peak of about 90 degrees and back down to 0 again. This wrist movement causes the rod to reposition the line closer to the angler. Additionally, the rod maneuvers through a half circle, (180 degree arc), as viewed by the angler.

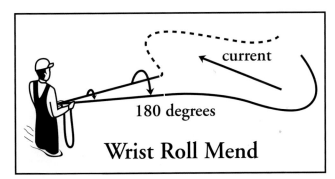

Wrist Roll Mend

Roll Mend

The roll mend produces more line movement than the standard wrist roll mend. This roll mend calls for adding

additional slack line by rod shaking. Next, gently elevate the rod tip, and finally make a small roll cast causing a little hoop of line to roll ahead repositioning the line belly into the desired position. This roll mend is of benefit when fishing faster currents.

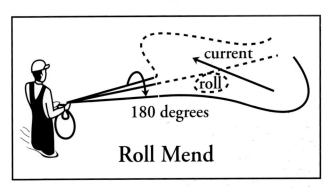

Roll Mend

Shoot Mend

The shoot mend is implemented in waters with current traps such as dead spots, swirls, and up dwellings. These spots catch the line belly, and the shoot mend frees the line from these traps.

The wrist and rod motion is identical to the wrist roll mend. The only difference is that a loop of line held by the line hand is shot during the mend. This repositions the mended line past the current trap. Additionally, the rod may need to be extended upwards and outwards while the mended line drifts past the current trap.

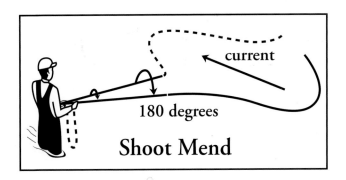

Shoot Mend

Still Water Dead Drift

Simply cast to the desired target area and strip in the excess slack line; carefully watch the fly. Some animation is helpful and is furnished by a "sudden inch" struggling movement. One or two quick hand twist retrieves can cause the fly to suddenly move

several inches and animate the fly's hackles by disturbing the surface film; furthermore, this action draws attention to the fly. An intermittent longer movement of about six inches followed by a pause is productive. To avoid unnatural motions keep in direct contact with the fly by allowing only a slight amount of slack line.

During windy times an intermediate sink rate line is more useful; it settles just below the surface and is not blown around as much as a floating line.

When cruising fish are present, notice their direction of travel and the cast is made to anticipate their next feeding site. This is perplexing because the fish move in irregular patterns rather than in straight lines. Envision the feeding pattern and rhythm. Estimate the next rise location by extrapolating from past rises. Once the cast is made, animate the fly a little to draw attention. Then stop and watch for the rise.

Feeding Lanes

A feeding lane is defined as the horizontal extent a fish will move to feed during an insect emergence. A feeding lane's width varies according to the following factors: hatch intensity, fish's size, and fish's dominance. These factors and some general rules will be discussed.

During an intense hatch, such as a trico spinner fall or a blue wing olive emergence, the feeding lanes may become as narrow as 1 or 2 inches in width. A sporadic hatch, such as callibaetis or green drake, may have a much wider feeding lane in excess of 3 feet. This wide variance is linked to the fish's need to collect the most nutrition with the least amount of energy expenditure. Catching a large green drake merits a longer swim than a tiny trico spinner does.

A fish's size may determine the feeding lane's width. Young, smaller fish tend to have wider feeding lanes than older larger fish. This is due to the fish's experience in energy conservation. An inexperienced fish may pursue every food item without regard to energy expenditure. Also, a smaller fish doesn't burn up as many calories in catching the same sized insect as a larger fish does. Hence, small fish can feed in wider lanes while larger fish have learned to select productive, narrow lanes in food gathering.

Dominant fish will seek out and overtake the best feeding spots. These positions have access to narrow efficient feeding lanes.

With intimidation, submissive fish are forced to feed in less productive lies which have wider feeding lanes. Consequently, the general rules are that the largest and most dominant fish will occupy the prime feeding lies where they can easily feed from the narrowest feeding lanes. Also, the quantity of available foods can decide the width of the feeding lane. A prime feeding lie is the most efficient feeding area. Here the greatest quantity of insects can be caught with the least amount of work.

With a wider feeding lane the fish must hold deeper. This depth is required because the vision window must be large enough to view the feeding lane. Conversely, shallow holding fish can only view narrow feeding lanes. These factors affect your approach because they influence a fish's vision and wariness. The size of the feeding lane affects your presentation. The narrower the lanes the more accurate your cast must be to place your fly within this lane. Take a moment and observe a feeding fish to see how far it will venture to catch an insect. Adjust your presentation accordingly.

Wet Fly Methods

Wet Fly Swing

The wet fly swing is used to present the fly in large riffles. Whenever the lie of a fish is uncertain, the wet fly swing system is helpful in discovering secluded fish. Nearly all of a riffle can be covered by adding a step-down between casts. It is a productive manner to fish both attractor and baitfish flies; furthermore, it's a favored steelhead method. The fly's swing conveys a lifelike appearance to its materials. With the wet fly swing both the surface and the depths of a run can be covered. A floating line is chosen to cover the surface while a sinking tip line is engaged to fish the bottom. The wet fly swing is performed as follows:

1. The cast is made slightly quartering downstream.
2. The line is mended as necessary to either slow or speedup the fly's drift. The mend's direction relies upon the current's mixed velocities in relation to the fly and line.
3. As the fly swings through its arc, track the fly's movement with the rod tip.

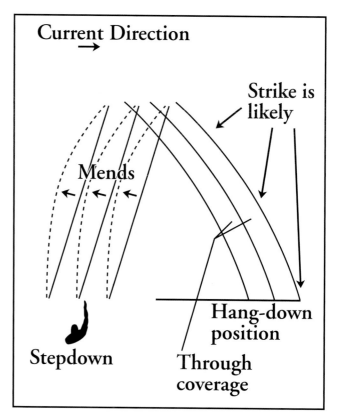

4. When the fly's swing ceases at the hang-down position, jig the fly and pause it to excite a strike from a following fish.
5. Step downstream a predetermined distance then recast the fly for the next presentation. This step-down provides the thorough coverage of the wet fly swing.

Modified Wet Fly Swing

The modified wet fly swing is adjusted to fish weighted flies or sink-tip lines along the stream's bottom. The modification is that the cast is directed three-quarters upstream instead of slightly downstream; this change permits the fly and line to sink deeper. Otherwise, this technique is identical to the wet fly swing with perhaps the additional need for some line mends. Swinging deeply through its arc, the fly is presented along the stream's bottom.

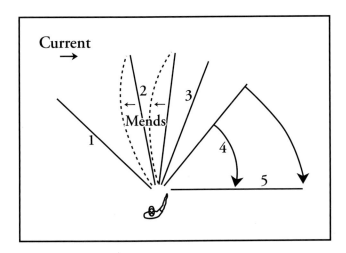

1. Cast 3/4 upstream.
2. Mends are made as necessary in the appropriate direction. These mends help sink the fly deeper because mending prevents line drag from pulling upwards on the fly.
3. When the fly is directly across the stream it has sunk to its deepest position.
4. Additionally, line may be played out to maintain the fly's depth and to retard the swing of the fly.
5. Retrieve sufficient line so the cast can be remade. Stepping down a given distance presents the fly to a different area.

The step-down distance is adjusted to exact stream conditions such as: feeding lane size, water clarity, temperature and light intensity. For example, when conditions favor inactive fish, the step-down distance is made shorter (perhaps only a foot or two); conversely, when conditions favor active fish the step-down distance is made longer (perhaps three to eight feet). In this way efficient presentations are made to thoroughly fish large riffles or holds.

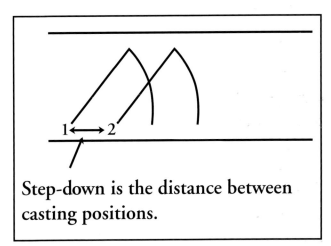

Step-down is the distance between casting positions.

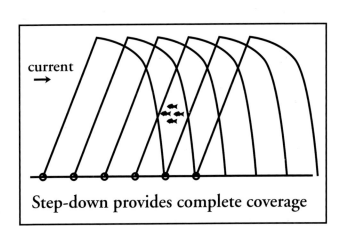

Step-down provides complete coverage

Lead Core Wet Fly Swing

An additional modification of the wet fly swing is employed to accommodate the greatest density lines, such as lead core and deep water express. With ease, the line is cast quartering downstream. Fewer line mends are needed to reach the swing down area.

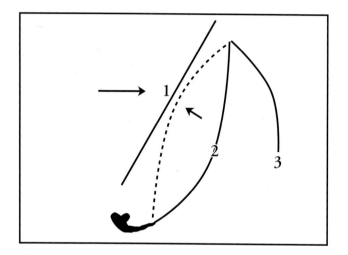

1. Cast is made 1/4 downstream.
2. A line mend or two may be used to slow the fly's descent.
3. As the fly swings to the hang-down position, enticingly jig and pause it to provoke a strike from a possible reluctant fish. Step-down and then recast the fly.

The highest density lines are lead core, deep water express, and Teeny series lines. Normally these come in either sink tip or shooting head lines. Their superb sinking qualities allow them to sink quickly, and this property saves time in getting the fly to the productive swing area. The ideal presentation is to suspend the fly just above the fish, because here it is easier for the fish to see and to strike the fly.

Riffling Hitch, Waking Fly

The riffling hitch provides a surface struggling-and-waking action that simulates an injured baitfish trying to right itself. With this crippled action, fish are attracted to an easily caught meal.

This method is productive for both salmon and steelhead as well as trout and smallmouth bass. Whenever the fish are actively feeding at the surface, the riffled fly may be fruitful. At times of giant stonefly and golden stonefly egg laying flights, the riffle hitch affords an enticing action. Stoneflies commonly sputter along at the surface during egg-laying.

Simply, the riffling hitch is just a couple of half-hitches tied to the head of the fly so that the leader extends out at a right angle. Using stiff heavy tippet materials accentuates the fly's action. The tippet can be tied to extend out on the right side, the left side, or the underneath side of the fly's head. Each position furnishes a different action when fished across the current. Frequently, the most useful hitch is the one that directs the tippet out towards the bank side of the fly when the fly is directed upstream. This position intensifies the fly's surface action. (See Diagram 6)

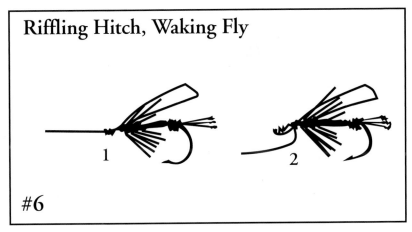

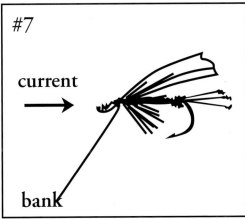

Riffling Hitch, Waking Fly

1

2

#6

#7

current

bank

1. Tippet is attached by an improved clinch knot.
2. To re-direct the tippet, two half hitches are placed out at a right angle to the fly's shank. These half-hitches are tied onto the fly's head.

The preferred riffle hitch bank position in relation to both the current's direction and the bank's position is to have the tippet extend out towards the bank when the fly's head is directed upstream. (See Diagram 7) The key to fishing the riffling hitch is to fish the fly under tension while it swings across the surface. (See Diagram 8)

1. Cast directly across stream.
2. Using several mends, slow or speed up the fly's descent while maintaining some direct line tension to the fly.
3. As the fly swings through the arch, watch for a possible strike. Many times interested fish may show themselves by boiling the surface.
4. Fish the drop down area by jigging and pausing the fly to entice any reluctant fish. Next step-down and recast the fly; in this way the entire

surface is fished. The choice of a fly pattern influences the fly's waking action. Flies tied with Muddler minnow head styles or with stiff hackles and hairs generate more surface disturbances. Additionally, waking flies should be tied with buoyant materials to help keep them afloat.

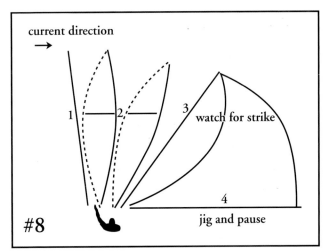

current direction

1 2 3 watch for strike

4
jig and pause

#8

Grease Line Presentation

The grease line presentation furnishes a broadside drift of the fly making the fly's wide silhouette more visible to the fish. The stream currents playing upon the fly materials make it come alive as it drifts downstream. During the drift the fly is fished in a drag-free manner, and then as it comes to the swing-down position it's fished the same as the wet fly swing. This grease line presentation was established long ago in Europe as an Atlantic salmon technique. The grease line refers to greasing or waterproofing the old silk lines to make them float.

Today the grease line is a very productive method for steelhead, salmon, trout, and other stream fish. It fishes efficiently both attractor and streamer fly patterns.

Originally used for fishing the surface, the grease line method can be adapted for fishing deep by using sink tip lines. With the stream's velocity in mind, the fly's materials are selected. Soft materials, such as marabou, are used in slower currents; stiff materials, such as bucktail, are used in faster currents; The key is to select a fly pattern which seductively moves with the current. Procedure: (See Diagram 9)

1. Cast is made quartering somewhat upstream.
2. Line mends are used to generate a drag-free broadside presentation. Properly timed and placed mends are essential to the success of the grease line presentation.
3. Optimal line tension is sustained to keep the fly drifting broadside. Maintaining a fairly straight or a slightly curved line affords sufficient tension to keep the fly oriented broadside.
4. At the end of drift the fly is fished the same as the wet fly swing. Enticingly jig and pause the fly at hang-down position before recasting.
5. The step-down procedure is employed to insure complete coverage of the riffle or run.

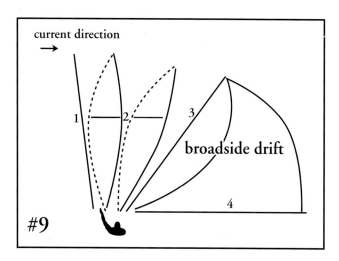

current direction

1 2 3
broadside drift
4
#9

In summary, this grease line presentation calls for exacting line mending techniques. The prime advantage over other swing techniques is that it provides the fish a better view of the broadside of the fly; additionally, an injured prey is simulated which may provoke a strike. This method is my favorite wet fly swing presentation. Moreover, sink tip lines permit deep coverage which adds the same advantages of enhanced visibility and crippled prey.

Strike Indicator - Nymph Fishing

Nymphs are effectively fished in a natural dead drift motion just above the stream's bottom structure. Here the current velocity is much slower than at its surface. Most nymphs are very poor swimmers and drift helplessly with the flow.

The angler's goal is to choose the optimal amount of weight to both place the nymph just above the stream's bottom and to match the current's velocity. My favorite terminal tackle consists of a long, somewhat thin leader, a strike indicator, two nymphs (tied on short droppers), and removable split shot.

The strike indicators can be a corkie (attached with a broken toothpick), yarn (dressed with fly floatant), closed cell foam (attached with a ring), or one of the many other commercial strike indicators. No matter which indicator you choose, it should be easily moved and firmly attached to the leader.

Removable shot is used so that the amount of weight can be quickly adjusted to the stream's depth and flow. The optimal amount of shot matches the current's actual flow rate at the depth that the nymph is being fished. This speed is always slower than the speed at the surface. (See Figure 10)

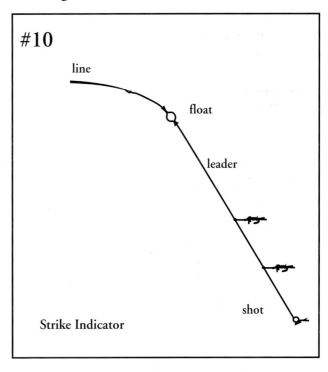

#10

line

float

leader

shot

Strike Indicator

A general rule is to adjust the weight so that the indicator is flowing more slowly than the surface bubbles and flotsam; usually one half of the surface speed matches the bottom speed. The shot is in direct contact with the bottom and is bouncing along in a tapping motion. When the strike-indicator hesitates or moves laterally or goes under, pull the rod in a downstream sweep. If a fish is felt, strike firmly to set the hook. With practice you can feel the difference between a snag and a fish. The key is to instantly set the hook when the strike indicator gives notice.

Nymph fishing is my method of choice at times of no insect hatches or emergences. Fish are foraging during these lean times and are usually not as selective as when a hatch is occurring. A well presented nymph usually results in an immediate strike. The underwater feeding lanes may vary in accordance with temperature, flow rate, and water clarity. Try to completely cover all of the possible holding lies where a fish may be found.

At times of insect emergence the fish can become selective and the emerging insects must be closely matched. At times of non-emergence, a variety of nymphs native to the stream can be effective.

Other terminal tackle set ups are also effective. Instead of shot, a weighted fly can be used. Here the fly acts as the weight and sinks into the desired depth.

The problem with the weighted fly is that it's difficult to adjust its weight to effectively fish various lies with different flows.

Bead-head nymphs are heavier than non-bead-head flies. Wraps of lead or copper wire can be tied underneath the fly.

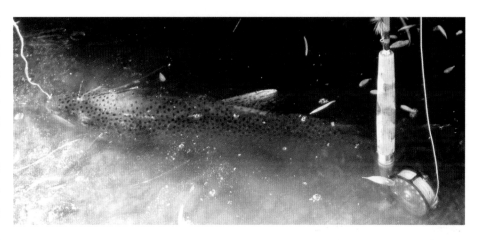

Adding shot above the fly can cause it to ride too close to the stream's bottom, making it more snag prone and less visible to the fish.

Lift

At the end of the fly's drift, raise the rod high and let the current pull the fly up to the surface. This imitates the rising emergence of an insect. It is simple to do and effective. The fish targets on the nymph's rising action. Mayflies and caddisflies are effectively fished with this lift method.

During insect emergence, fish often feed upon the nymphs transforming into adults. Fish can become selective and prefer eating these helpless emergent nymphs rather than the mature adults. Adult flies can flutter and this movement makes it difficult for a fish to catch them. Some fish, during heavy insect hatches, specialize in feeding upon the transforming nymphs and the cripples. These fish can ignore the moving adult insects. Carefully observe rising fish to see what insect life stage is being ingested.

Surface film nymphs are fished the same as dry fly presentations. That is upstream, 7/8, natural drift, Young's, and all of the downstream presentations. Simply fish the nymph the same as the dry fly.

Streamers

Streamers are effectively fished by combining a strip or a pull retrieve with the wet fly swing, grease line, modified wet fly swing, or lead core swing. Sometimes the skating retrieve is used.

The strip retrieve is used to move the fly a short distance while the pull retrieve allows the fly to move a longer distance. The rates of both retrieves are adjusted to match the activity level of the bait fish.

Sculpins are bottom dwellers that move from one bottom area to another. My favorite retrieve in imitating this motion is done as follows. Simply use the pull retrieve but release the line back into the water instead of retrieving it. The line hand holds the line in the same place during the retrieve. This allows the fly slack line so that it sinks to a new bottom area. The fly will sort of yo-yo through the retrieve. Your sculpin imitation needs to be weighted in its thorax area to do this. Cast 3/4 upstream, allow fly to sink to the bottom,

and then pull in about 2-3 feet of line as the fly drifts downstream. Take your line hand and move it towards your stripping guide. Your line hand doesn't release the line. This causes a series of 2-3 foot pulls and 2-3 foot releases. The sculpin's action is that it lifts off the bottom and settles back to the bottom as it drifts through the presentation. The strike is usually a violent one requiring little hook setting.

Caddisflies

Adult caddisflies are very active. After hatching they can live for about 3 weeks. At low light they dance on the river's surface. Perhaps they are either drinking or laying eggs. Whether they are drinking or laying eggs, they skitter the surface in erratic flight patterns. Fish love them.

I fish them in an active skating retrieve combined with an assortment of presentations. The classic upstream, Young's method, and the downstream presentations are effective. I prefer to fish 2 flies. One is an exact size and the other is one size larger than the naturals. I fish the smaller pattern on the dropper which is about 2-3 feet away from the larger fly. My favorite patterns are the elk hair caddis ones treated with fly floatant. (Gink etc.)

This skating method is explained in the retrieves chapter. I exaggerate the motions so that the dropper fly lifts off of the water a few inches and splashes back down. The larger fly actively disturbs the surface. This presentation and retrieve elicits aggressive surface rises. I have found it to be effective even when the caddisflies are not active such as in bright sunlight. This method, fished next to bank side shadows, can entice inactive fish into feeding. When used in low light conditions when lots of caddisflies are active, it can be extremely effective.

I prefer the Young's method for this skating technique. I allow the flies to be active and then float freely for a short distance. This activity attracts fish to your flies.

RETRIEVES 6

A broad range of retrieves is needed to simulate the natural motions of aquatic foods. Insects possess a variety of means of locomotion. Some foods move slowly while others are much faster. Likewise, aquatic insects display a wide variance in their motions.

A fish is fooled when a fly both looks and acts lifelike. The importance of the correct retrieve which simulates the natural motions of the insect coupled with a fly pattern matching color, size, shape, and silhouette of the insect will be deadly.

Most of the time in lake fishing the goal is to present the fly just above the bottom. This is achieved by taking into account the line's sink rate, suspension depth, and allotted sinking time. Adjust these factors to place the fly precisely at the optimal depth.

The retrieve is accomplished by a combination of rod and line hand movements. The basic hand position prepares you to both properly retrieve the fly and to battle the fish. The hook set and fight take place immediately during the retrieve. The basic rod hand position when rod movement is not part of the retrieve is as follows: The rod hand grasps the cork grip in the normal casting position with the thumb extended on top of the cork and the index finger directly below it. Either the index or the middle finger controls the line by acting as a guide and a brake that can pinch off the line against the cork. I prefer the middle finger to act as the line guide and brake because it leaves the thumb and index finger in control of a firm rod grip. Additionally, the ring finger can assist in pressing the line against the grip. By applying slight finger pressure, a line drag can be instantly applied and adjusted. The line finger plays a role in both fighting a fish and making the retrieve. With much practice this line finger can become proficient as an instant judge of drag tension. Most of the time, I employ the lightest drag pressure setting on my reel (just light enough to prevent a spool overrun). Next, I rely upon my fingers to apply additional pressure to the line and reel spool. This gives me an instant feel for what an unpredictable fish is doing. The finger drag control is useful in nearly all freshwater angling.

A retrieve's basic rod position is to point the rod downwards toward the line and the fly. The rod tip can be submerged.

The basic retrieves are the strip, pull, and hand twist. Each will be discussed.

Basic Hand Position

Strip Retrieve

The line is grasped between the thumb and first finger of the line hand and stripped in a down and backward motion. Next, release the grasp on the line and return the line hand back to its original position. The length and speed of this strip can be varied. The rod hand's line finger acts as a line guide and as a brake for a sudden stop in the retrieve or in firmly striking a fish. This retrieve is most commonly used to imitate a wide variety of prey.

Strip Retrieve is executed as shown in A-C

Pull Retrieve

The pull retrieve shares the same basic hand positions as the strip retrieve; however, it differs in that the line is pulled back in a much longer direction with the line hand extending back posteriorly. This pull retrieve is suitable for both long slow or fast retrieves. It is commonly used to imitate baitfish.

A Pull Retrieve is executed as shown in A & B

Hand Twist

The hand twist retrieve is done by grasping the line between the line hand's thumb and first two fingers and pulling an inch or two of line into the palm of your hand. Next, drop the pulled line and rotate the wrist so your fingers are back in the original position and repeat this procedure by grasping the line again. This retrieve is useful in making slow erratic motions; it imitates the majority of small aquatic food sources.

The distinguishing features between these basic retrieves are the distance that the fly moves. The speed can be varied for each. The longest of the retrieves is the pull. The intermediate one is the strip and the shortest one is the hand twist. Perhaps the strip retrieve is the most useful because it can provide the widest range of motions. The hand twist is best at making a short erratic motion; the pull can advance the fly for the longest distance.

Retrieve combinations are useful in mimicking the natural motions of insects and baitfish. Modifying these three basic retrieves can cause the fly to crawl, creep, pause, or move in steady, quick, erratic or twitching movements. The key is to match the retrieve to the natural motion of the insect you are imitating. The basic retrieve combinations are: sink-and-draw, lift-off-and-settle, rise-and-fall, wind drift, countdown, and skating. These retrieves are useful in still waters and in some slow current conditions.

The Hand Twist Retrieve is executed as shown in A-E

Sink-and-Draw

The sink-and-draw retrieve is accomplished by allowing the fly to sink to the desired depth and then by retrieving upwards toward the surface. Hatching insects naturally migrate toward the surface so this sink-and-draw retrieve simulates this action.

Take into account the bottom's contour by casting from the shallows toward the depths, or this retrieve can be used by casting parallel to the bottom's general contours. The speed of the retrieve is matched to suspend the fly within a foot of the bottom. The retrieve is accelerated to raise the fly to the surface, and stopped or slowed to sink back down again. Both the line's sink rate and the retrieve rates are the factors that suspend the fly at the desired depths. When the sink-and-draw retrieve is used with a floating line and an increased retrieve rate, the fly will rise toward the surface. Emerging insects move in this same manner. When using a floating line and a long leader, the fly is allowed to sink to the bottom. As the retrieve starts, the fly rises from the bottom and becomes readily visible to the fish. Its pathway to the surface simulates an emerging insect. The fly needs to be optimally weighted; that is, heavy enough to sink it and the long leader to the bottom but still light enough to move upwards toward the surface when retrieved. A fly tied on a heavy wet fly hook with sparse webby hackles and a fur dubbing will usually suffice. Sometimes a few turns of fine lead wire may be needed to weight the fly enough for it to sink. Fluorocarbon leaders are denser and easier to sink than monofilament ones. The emerging motion of the midge or caddis pupa is well mimicked by the sink-and-draw retrieve.

Lift-Off-and-Settle

As an insect migrates toward the surface it may tire en route and settle back down to rest. The travel direction is an upwards and downwards motion that eventually reaches the surface. When insects are preparing for hatching they become active, performing many false starts and stops; this occurs for about one hour before actual emergence. The insect's increased activity lifts them off the bottom and makes them both visible and available to the fish. An effective technique is to fish the lift-off-and-settle retrieve from a boat or a float tube. A standard hook fly pattern retrieved over a relatively clean bottom fishes well; on the other hand, weedy bottoms may require a weedless fly pattern to prevent snagging. This retrieve is achieved by casting the fly to the desired position and allowing it to sink to the bottom. Next, the lift-off is made by lifting the rod tip upwards and the settle is done by immediately lowering the rod tip back down. Strip in the slack line with the line hand. Continue this action until the fly is completely retrieved.

Strikes may occur at any time. Be prepared for either soft or hard strikes. The slightest line resistance on either the rise or the fall portions of the retrieve may be a soft strike. Also, during the lifting phase strikes can become arm-wrenching affairs.

Rise-and-Fall

The rise-and-fall retrieve differs from the lift-off-and-settle in that the rise-and-fall "s" motion is of less magnitude. It is best used to imitate insects that tire and settle back down to rest. A damselfly's vigorous abdominal motions are energy consuming and tiring. These nymphs need frequent rest stops and during these pauses the nymphs sink. Also, scud's and water boatmen's motions are well mimicked by this rise-and-fall retrieve.

A slightly weighted fly paired with either a floating or a short sinking tip line is used depending upon water depth. A floating line is used for the shallower waters while sinking lines are used for deeper waters.

Simply allow the fly to sink and retrieve it toward the surface with a slow strip retrieve. Next, stop the retrieve and allow it to sink back again.

Wind-Drift

The wind-drift retrieve uses the motion of a lake's surface ripples and waves to vertically move the fly. Additionally, a boat's or float tube's wind-drift advances the fly horizontally. A 90 degree cast into the wind allows both you and the fly to horizontally move at about the same rate. A floating line is used because the wave action is limited only to the surface and the depths are sheltered from this action. You simply wind-drift through the desirable locations. Your motion is silent and concealed because the rippled surface allows a quiet, close approach that doesn't alarm the fish. A sinking line is used to troll through an area by wind-drift. The fly can be given added motions by lifting and dropping the rod; also, the wave action affords it some natural-like animation.

An alternate method is to strip and release line for the stop and go motion. It is imperative to select the optimal sinking density line to suspend your offering just over the bottom.

Both methods are great searching techniques. When fish are found, return to their location and concentrate your efforts there. Dry flies drifted through foam lines are especially effective. Callibaetis spinners are effectively fished by wind-drift.

Countdown

Perhaps the countdown retrieve is the most valuable still water technique. This retrieve purposefully presents your fly at the desired depth for the longest time. Fishing just above submerged weed beds is perhaps the most effective still water technique. To insure that your fly will be presented at the proper depth, match the fly line's sinking rate to the depth of the submerged weed beds. This depth can be detected by probing a marked line and weight or by the use of video sonar. Sinking lines are available in the following densities: intermediate, 1, 2,

3, 4, 5, and 6. Each line sinks at a faster rate as its number increases. Sinking lines suspend themselves at an approximate depth. The following table provides the suspension depths.

Line	Suspension Depth
Intermediate	0-5 ft.
1. slow	5-10 ft.
2. fast	8-20 ft.
3. hi-density	20-30 ft.
4. hi-speed	25-35 ft.
5. V	30-40 ft.
6. VI	35 ft.

In the countdown method the cast is completed and the line is pulled straight. Next, a timed count is made to allow the line to sink to the desired depth. It is an advantage to select a line that will suspend itself at the desired depth.

For example, a 12 ft. deep submerged weed bed is fished with a wet cell 2 sink rate line. In about 36 seconds the line sinks to about the 11 ft. depth; here it suspends itself by slowing its sinking rate. At this depth the line's specific gravity approaches the water volume that it displaces. A timed count of 36 seconds is made and adjusted by trial and error until the line sinks to the desired depth. At first you may deliberately over count the sinking time, then attune the count until you no longer snag weeds. The same type 2 line used in a six-foot depth will continue to sink and have a tendency to hang up in the weeds. Here, in six-foot depths, a wet cell 1 line is an in-between choice because it starts suspending at the six-foot depth. Its slowed sinking rate allows a longer retrieve without hanging up on weeds. The best line choice is made by selecting the slowest sink rate that will reach the desired depth. Success depends upon the line selection. Suspended flies at the fish's depth can be fished for a greater distance and time. This simply boosts your odds of catching fish.

In lake fishing the line selection is more important than the fly selection. You must present your offering to the fish.

Skating

Skating a fly over the surface can attract fish from a larger area. Making the fly hop, skip, and skitter are desirable motions. Adult caddisflies and damselflies routinely skate the surface; likewise, threatened baitfish skip the surface in an effort to avoid capture by predators. Skating is a natural motion for some aquatic foods.

A skating retrieve is done by using both the rod and line hands in a coordinated effort. The line hand retrieves long fast strips of line while the rod hand pulses the rod in a fast up-and-down motion. This causes the fly to skip along the surface. The rod's vibrations cause tantalizing pulsations. The stripping moves the fly along the surface.

This pulsating action can be irresistible to fish; consequently, strikes can be so savage that all you need to set the hook is to make solid contact. Because of these violent strikes, heavy tippets are preferred over fine ones.

Fly pattern choices should be exceptionally high floating ones tied with plenty of hollow deer or elk hair. Bullet head fly designs amplify the pulses.

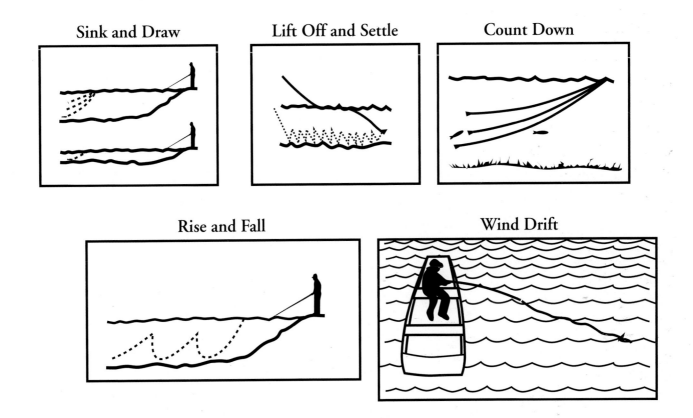

Sink and Draw

Lift Off and Settle

Count Down

Rise and Fall

Wind Drift

Summary

The most common error is to overdo the retrieve by making the motions excessively fast and long. Insects are small and their motions are subtle; moreover, they proceed for shorter distances and at a slower rate than fishermen envision.

Carefully observe the natural insect's or baitfish's motions. Copy this action. Most retrieves are best done with a slower-than-you-think rate and distance. Some exceptions are threatened baitfish and adult caddisflies. But most other aquatic foods require subtle retrieves.

Many fishermen retrieve their flies in 3 to 4 foot pulls; but the naturals move only an inch or so and cannot possibly swim in sudden 3 foot spurts.

Your primary retrieve goal is to copy the naturals' motions in both rate and distance.

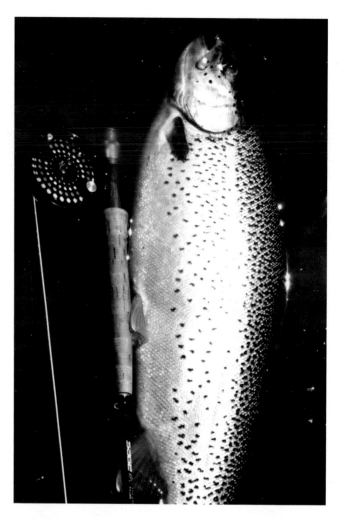

Table of Retrieves

Aquatic Food	Distance	Rate	Retrieve
Water Boatman	2"-6"	erratic stop and go	hand twist, sink & draw
Sculpins	1'-3'	slow & moderate	strip/ rise & fall
Stoneflies (adults)	3"-12"	erratic fluttering	strip
Stoneflies (nymphs)	dead drift	slow shoreward crawl	hand twist
Damselflies (adults)	3"-24"	fast skittering	skating
Damselflies (nymphs)	3"-6"	slow stop & go	hand twist
Dragonflies (adults)	same as damselflies		
Dragonflies (nymphs)	3"-12"	fast, short, stop & go	strip
Leeches	3"-12"	moderate stop & go	strip
Snails	motionless	use short pull then stop	strip
Eggs	none	none	strip to gain attention then stop
Crayfish	6"-18"	fast stop & go	strip
Scuds/sow bugs	1", 3"-6"	erratic stop & go	hand twist
Baitfish	3"-6"-36"	moderate & fast	strip or pull
Hoppers/crickets	1-3"	erratic	hand twist
Beetles/ants	1-3"	varied	strip
Shrimp	2"-12"	varied	strip
Caddis flies	3"-12"	erratic fast	strip or skating
Mayflies	0-6"	dead drift & take off	hand twist or strip

7
STREAM CHARACTERISTICS

Streams are classified into three basic categories: spring creek, freestone, and tail water streams. Each type has unique features.

Spring Creeks

A spring creek originates from an underground source—a spring. Because of their gentle gradients, spring creeks are generally flat and smooth; they are found in valley floors rather than in steep canyons.

A spring creek's underground water source produces a constant flow volume, and seasonal variances are slight. Usually spring creeks are not subject to the high runoffs which erode out the streambed channel. Instead, spring creeks have stable flows and streambed channels.

Rooted aquatic plants favor spring creeks because they are free to grow, sheltered from the scouring of high water flows. This allows plants to grow extensive rooted weed beds which provide prime habitat for both aquatic insects and fish. The enhanced surface areas of the leaves and stems support an abundance of hiding places for insects to live and feed. Fish devour these insects.

Spring creeks are generally slightly alkaline in nature. This basic pH range favors plant, insect, and fish growth. A spring creek's underground water source filters through carbonates and alkaline elements enriching its water quality.

Spring creeks have stable temperatures. The ground flows arise at a constant year-round temperature which is generally between 50-55°F. The spring's temperature is not influenced by its downstream

climatic conditions. This is a year-round advantage because the energy required to alter the core temperature of a large volume of water is great. For instance, in the wintertime a spring creek enjoys warmer temperatures than its surroundings and in the summertime a spring creek savors cooler temperatures. Hence a spring creek's extended growing season favors fish because they are insulated from severe temperature variances. Much of the year a spring creek's temperature is near the preferred range for fish growth.

At times of extreme hot or cold weather, fish seek refuge in the proximity of a spring creek's source. Here the fish are sheltered from winterkill or summer heat die-offs.

In short, a spring creek's favorable conditions of constant flows, optimal alkalinity, abundant vegetation, and stable temperatures all contribute to enhanced fish production. The only disadvantage I've found is that spring creeks are somewhat scarce and the good ones have already been discovered. Their reputations make them popular angler destinations resulting in crowded fishing. Just visit Idaho's Harriman Park during its green drake hatch and you will be amazed at its popularity. Some spring creeks require reservations.

Freestone Streams

A freestone stream's water source is either snowmelt or rainfall, so they rely upon precipitation for their flow volume. Freestones generally have steep gradients characterized by areas of rapid and fast currents. They are usually sited in canyon areas.

A freestone stream's volume crests in early summer while its flow diminishes in the fall and winter. The stark contrast between late springtime and winter flows can be surprising. A once productive summer side-channel may be bone dry in the winter. Springtime flows may be high and muddy yet run low and clear the rest of the season. High flows commonly scour stream channels. Rooted aquatic plants have difficulty surviving the seasonal heavy flows. Stream channels can change from one year to the next. Some scouring may be beneficial if it washes away excess silt accumulated in the rocky, gravelly, riffled sections. Freestones are distinguished by few rooted aquatic plants and by an abundance of gravel and rocks.

Aquatic insects require plants to exist. Riffles support sheltered areas for limited plant growth. Aquatic insects live and feed in the riffled areas where the enhanced surface areas between the rocks support plant habitat. Hence, the riffles provide the freestone stream with its abundance of

aquatic insects for the fish to forage.

A freestone stream's pH is usually slightly acidic. In times of excess acid, plants, insects, and fish may perish. The snow pack at a stream's source can accumulate acidic precipitation. This is concentrated into the bottom layer of snow. As this bottom layer melts, the sudden release of acid can be devastating to its downstream environment.

A freestone stream is more readily influenced by the ambient air temperature, resulting in wide temperature fluctuations. Winter cold can cause a stream to run close to freezing while summer heat can cause it to exceed 70°F. This wide variation shortens a fish's growing season which occurs when

the water temperature is between 55-65 degrees. The lowered winter and late summer diminished water volume is more easily influenced by ambient temperature changes. Conditions of bottom ice along with an ice lid surface can induce winter kill of both insects and fish. Likewise, summer die-offs occur due to excessively warm temperatures which forfeit water's ability to hold sufficient oxygen.

The productive freestone streams are restricted to ideal altitudes and latitudes where seasonal temperatures are favorable for aquatic life.

As a general rule, the freestone stream's growing season is much shorter than a spring creek's, because freestones are more prone to wide temperature fluctuations.

In summary, freestones are subject to times of plenty and to times of drought. They are not as rich in food resources as spring creeks. Their grace is that freestones are wider, longer, and more numerous than spring creeks. Nonetheless, freestones are less crowded than spring creeks. Since freestones have fewer fish than a spring creek, an angler must cover more water in search of fish.

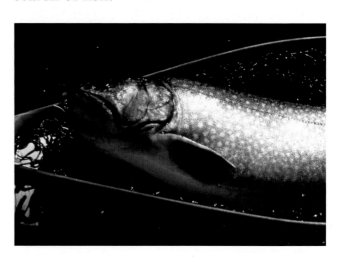

Tail Water Streams

Tail water streams are found below dams and their water source flows from the reservoir. The outlet comes from controlled head gates which release water out from the bottom of the dam; as a result, the most dense and coldest water is released. It is typically around 39-40°F. At flood times, water can be released over the dam's safety spillway. This water is derived from the reservoir, and contains the warmest, least dense water. Occasionally a reservoir is designed to purposely release water from any of its depths. For example, Utah's Flaming Gorge regulates its outlet flows by adjustable baffles set to expel more favorably temperatured water. Its outlet, the Green River, is optimally controlled to provide water temperatures most suited for aquatic life. The Green River is more like a large spring creek in that its flow is optimal for fish growth. This good fortune has made it a highly productive fishery, although most other tail waters are not so lucky.

The basic problem of most tail waters is that below their dams they are just too cold for optimal fish growth. Conditions can become more favorable the farther downstream you travel from the dam's head gates. The ambient temperature warms the chilly flows.

Dams are built for three general proposes: hydropower productions, irrigation and culinary storage, and flood control. Each of these dams has unique features.

Hydropower dams can be subject to daily variances in outlet flows. At peak electricity use times, more flow is released to generate power. This causes both a sudden temperature variation and flow alteration which can frustrate fishermen.

Irrigation dams are characterized by peak seasonal flows during the agriculture growing season and diminished flows during storage times. This results in prominent summer flows; summer channels may be left high and dry in the winter. These wide fluctuations support marginal fish habitat.

The dams built for flood control may be better suited for fish because they provide stable year round flows. During the winter months, water is released to make room for anticipated springtime flood storage capacity. This stable flow provides better fish habitat. The big plus in some tail waters is that they have created trout habitat where it didn't previously exist. Some of the better tail waters can simulate spring creeks. They have ideal flow volumes and stable temperatures. They are sheltered from high water erosion and they can cultivate rooted aquatic plants. These tail waters enjoy an abundance of plants, insects, and fish. The problem with tail waters is that not all are created equally, and only some support great habitat.

When I fish a freestone stream I can cover miles of it in a single day, making it a long walk back to the truck. On the other hand, I usually fish a much shorter stretch of a spring creek. The fly patterns, sizes, line weights, tippets, and rod actions vary somewhat for each stream type.

A Beginning Point

A beginning fly fisherman can learn much about fish habitat by fishing a small stream. First, select a stream with an abundance of naive fish; next, fish 100% of the stream. Take note of the places that hold fish and the places that do not. Nowadays, it's difficult to find such a stream. You may have to find one out in the backwoods. When I started fishing in the 1960's, such streams were somewhat abundant. I vividly recall fishing Utah's Wild Strawberry River which entailed descending a roadless canyon inhabited by mule deer, black bear, and an occasional rattlesnake. This stream had well defined holes, riffles, undercut banks, and pocket waters, and it was full of willing trout. I simply fished all this stream and I soon had an idea of where its best fish would be found. Try to find such a stream in your area and spend some time fishing it. Then use what you have learned on larger streams.

The following is a discussion of stream characteristics: riffles, current seams, prime lies, resting lies, feeding lies, deep holes, and dead waters. These will be described in an effort to help you identify them.

Riffles (Feeding Lies)

Riffles are places where the current picks up speed as it runs a relatively straight course over a gravelly or rocky bed. In freestone streams this rocky bed provides the most habitats for aquatic food production. The surface area created by the regular contoured bottom provides many places for aquatic plants to grow. It is the basketball and smaller sized rocks that provide the optimal number of places for plants. In turn, these plants generate the food chain for aquatic insects and other animals. The rocks cushion the current's flow and make places where fish can hold without fighting the current. Since the bulk of the food supply is in a riffle, fish like to hold as close to it as possible without having to expend excessive energy staying there. As a result fish seek the cushioned areas inside or adjacent to riffles.

Current Seams

My favorite riffle lies are the current seams created by junctures of fast and slow flows. Here the fish enjoy the best of both worlds: a cushioned lie with food drifting and depositing at its front door. Fish can rest in these seams and dart out into the adjacent riffle to capture prey and return back to rest in the seam. Current seams are formed by the nature of current flow. Usually the middle of a riffle contains the fastest flow with its edges having slower flows due to friction with the bank and the stream bed obstacles. A stream channel's curvature redirects its heaviest flow away from the remainder of the stream creating current seams. In addition, a riffle's surface reflects its stream bed contours. Riffles vary widely in both depth and speed resulting in a multitude of current seams which provide desired fish habitat.

A riffle's broken surface affords an overhead canopy which obstructs the vision of birds of prey. In this way riffles create protective cover.

The current velocity increases as the stream bed narrows; likewise, wide riffles have slower velocities.

A riffle's depth and speed play a role in its fish holding capability. Some are just too fast and deep for fish to hold in; therefore, look for the moderate and slower riffles to hold fish. Look for fish just above or below a basketball sized rock which creates a cushioned lie just right for fish.

The fastest current is at the surface of the water and it progressively slows down as it reaches its stream bed. The bottom obstructions further decrease the current speed, making favorable conditions for aquatic life.

At times when insects are hatching, fish migrate to these riffle areas to actively feed. Prior to hatching on the surface, emerging insects are active and exposed next to the stream bed.

Sunlight affects fish activities. A bright overhead sun can illuminate a riffle enough so that birds of prey can spot and sweep down upon fish. This alarms the fish and they avoid these shallows during bright light conditions. During low light periods fish migrate back to these shallow areas to feed in safety. My favorite conditions are overcast days in which fish feel safe and stay in the shallow riffles feeding throughout the day.

Fall, winter, and spring sunlight hits at a lowered angle and doesn't illuminate the water as well as a high angled summer sun. This causes fish to hold longer in the riffles during the off season.

A spring creek's feeding lies can be just about anywhere that there is an abundance of rooted aquatic plants. Perhaps the best lies are submerged plants because they produce an abundance of insects. Plants act like rocks in a freestone's riffle by cushioning the current's flow. Rarely will you encounter extensive weed beds in waters too swift for fish to hold. Look for weed beds and fish will be close by, especially during an insect hatch.

Pocket Water

Pocket waters are mini-resting lies located in the midst of water unsuitable to hold fish. Search for pockets in the middle of a fast riffle or in slow shallows; likewise, a snag caked with vegetation can provide protective cover even in the shallows. A large rock in the midst of fast water cushions its flow, creating a small holding lie. These areas can hold a few fish.

Pocket-holding fish are opportunistic feeders and they must make immediate feeding decisions. A wide variety of fly patterns tied in larger sizes can be effective. Attractor patterns are also effective.

I enjoy fishing pocket water because the first cast is the most effective one. Drift boat fishing puts you into a multitude of pocket lies where fast, accurate casts produce fish.

Water temperatures play a vital role in finding fish. Swift, cold flows are just too energy consuming for fish to hold in riffles. At times of more favorable temperatures, fish spread throughout a riffle to forage.

predation and current force. A deep hole's depth provides protection from predation and the current. Although many deep holes may lack an abundant food supply such as a riffle can provide, drifting food may still be deposited. Many times deep holes become daytime hiding places; at low light fish migrate to feed in the riffles. Tail outs of deep holes may contain a riffled area. Deeper holes directly downstream from shallow riffles can also become prime lies because emerging insects are delivered directly into these holes. An alarmed fish can quickly return to the depths of the hole for protection.

Prime Lies

Prime lies provide fish the best habitat by providing protection, food, and rest. Prime lies become homes for the largest and the most dominant fish. This habitat is typically created by an undercut bank with overhanging vegetation downstream from a food producing riffle. The overhead canopy shelters the fish from predation and the current's friction against the undercut bank and bottom rubble provides a cushion of relief out of the stream's force. A current seam is created inside this lie where riffle food is deposited.

Deep Holes

Deep holes are usually resting lies but some can also be considered prime lies. A resting lie awards protection from both

Structure

Structure is anything that furnishes holding cover. Logs and fallen trees enhance an area by providing cover. Structures cause current cushions and hiding places. A fallen tree can create a lie which astonishing numbers of fish can use. Structure may include a wide variety of objects such as roots, plants, rocks, fallen trees, and even abandoned car bodies. I once caught a huge brown trout that lived in the back seat of a submerged Buick. I think that even a bigger one lived in the trunk.

Resting Lies

Resting lies are cushioned places where fish can rest from the current's flow. Additional protective cover such as overhead vegetation or an increase in depth makes them more attractive for fish. Resting lies can lack a ready food supply and are usually distant from riffles. Fish seek resting spots during non-hatching and brightly lit conditions. Fish readily migrate out of resting lies during a hatch and subdued light. Since food can be scarce in resting lies, the fish may become opportunistic feeders. An attractor fly can be productive when fished in rest stops.

Dead Water

Dead water refers to wide expanses of shallow, muddy stream bed areas that are void of rooted plants. This habitat lacks the food production ability of a riffle. Heavily silted streams commonly harbor large areas of dead water. This is why watershed deterioration is so devastating to a stream. The silt deposits inside the riffles and destroys their insect-producing capacities. Dead waters also lack protective cover and are dangerous places for fish to hold. Most of the time dead waters lack

fish. Occasionally wind-blown insects may collect in these areas. Fish can migrate to them to feed upon accumulated dead or crippled insects, although these fish are overly alert and can be difficult to approach. During large hatches of small mayflies and heavy spinner falls, the wind can cause these insects to accumulate into dead waters.

Curvatures

Streambed curvatures form different types of fish holding places. The outside bends or greater curvatures receive the current's scouring actions. High flows cause a deepening of the riverbed channel. During low water conditions, holes and deep runs are present along with undercut

stream banks. These quickly become favored fish holding places.

The inside or lesser curvature induces deposition of items carried by the currents. Here away from the main flow, food items settle. In addition, drifting insects are concentrated here.

Current seams are found as junctures between swift and slow flows. These seams can become favored lies that continually hold fish. Seams occur at both the great and the lesser stream curvatures. Seams are created by the shearing between fast currents and slower currents.

Islands generate additional current seams. Fish prefer the island's seams because of a bonus of terrestrial insects coming from the island's vegetation. An island's placement provides a sort of wing foil with different current speeds on each side. The current seams occur on upstream sides, alongside, and downstream. The island's vegetation enhances its bank-side cover. Stream braiding further enhances both the number of current seams and the bank-

side cover. The placement of an upstream riffle generates an open refrigerator door with insect emergence settling down back to the island. My favorite streams have lots of islands and channels because these structures enhance the number of fish producing lies.

A single island produces at least four different current seams. Two of them are further enhanced by bank-side cover and undercut banks.

Even small islands with limited cover enhance the stream's habitat. Here, mini-current shears, channels, and undercutting provide pocket water lies.

Don't overlook small side channels in a large river system. But remember a prerequisite for productive habitat is a prior history of stable flows. It takes some time for fish to relocate if the minor channel has been recently dewatered.

Midstream

Fish may migrate to midstream areas when temperatures are high and oxygen content is low. Here the midstream's faster riffles and whitewaters mix oxygen into the water. Consequently, pockets and holding areas amidst the whitewater can attract fish.

Foam Lines

Foam lines are the surface accumulations of floating matter. Here stillborn, emerging, and drowned terrestrial insects are collected. The foam traps the insects and holds them in place. The surface tension along with the foam holds the insects. The foam creates an overhead canopy that protects the fish from bird predation. Also this canopy shades the sunlight; as a result, there are usually fish underneath a foam line.

Eddy Lines

Eddy lines peel off from the river's bends, points, and island heads; they provide comfortable lies for fish to hold. Their broken surfaces conceal feeding fish. Eddies are protected lies away from the current's scouring effects; as a result, rooted aquatic plants are able to grow and enhance the quality of insect life. Eddies provide both food and shelter for fish.

Edge Waters

Usually the shallow's edge waters with little cover appear to be devoid of fish. These areas can become feeding lies because hatched insects tend to collect in these slack currents. Here the stillborn and spent spinners concentrate; as a result, these insects can be easily caught by foraging fish.

Although fish in edge water areas are watchful for predators, they are only found here when the food supply is ample. An errant cast or a noisy approach can cause these fish to streak for cover. A trout hooked here can panic and its first run can be exciting. Look for edge water fish during times of abundant insect emergence. Both the winter midge hatches and the late summer small mayfly activities make edge waters good feeding lies.

Lesser Curvatures

The slower and shallower inside flows of a river bend can be productive habitat. Weed beds can flourish here providing both shelter and insects; furthermore, at times of abundant hatches, fish can prefer these locations. In big tail water streams, inside bends provide an immense area of productive water. Huge schools of fish can seek out these areas.

Fish feeding in inside bends can become highly selective. They see a limited assortment of food varieties and become accustomed to feeding upon what is hatching. In these calm waters fish can scrutinize the size, shape, color, and action of their feed; therefore, your fly must be properly matched and presented.

Another problem of inside bends is that the mini-turbulences caused by waving weed beds complicate a drag free presentation. Here use a careful presentation with a highly flexible leader tippet.

Fish can hold in these lies during non hatch periods. At these times fish tend to school tighter together in the deeper part of the stream's inside bend.

Strategy

Once a beginning flyfisherman has experienced these various lies on a small stream, he (she) is ready to fish the larger streams. Fish the larger stream as a group of small streams adjacent to each other. Locate the many feeding, resting, and prime lies and fish them just like you did on the small stream.

For example, Montana's Madison River can be intimidating to a novice. Ignore its heavy flows and focus on the first twenty feet of the bank side waters. Fish this just like your small stream. Look for current seams because these are prime lies that seem to always collect good fish. Take into account the light intensity, temperature, insect activity, and you will discover the best water to fish.

A large spring creek such as Idaho's Henry's Fork can be perplexing. Again, divide it up into small stream segments and look for the resting, feeding, and prime lies.

Huge coastal rivers such as Oregon's Rogue River can be puzzling with many heavy flows and deep currents that are nearly impossible to penetrate. Remember that anadromous fish must migrate upstream through this river's maze of rapids. Its

salmon and steelhead have hundreds of miles to migrate and must choose the easiest flows to navigate through. This means the fish are swimming upstream through the river's depths from knee to chest deep, and its current velocity is about as fast as you can walk. Eliminate all of the other water and concentrate your efforts on these fish migration paths. Again take into account the other factors which can influence fish activities. Look for resting lies and migratory highways. Spend your time fishing these areas.

Stream Characteristics Exposure

Tailwater

Spring creek

Freestone

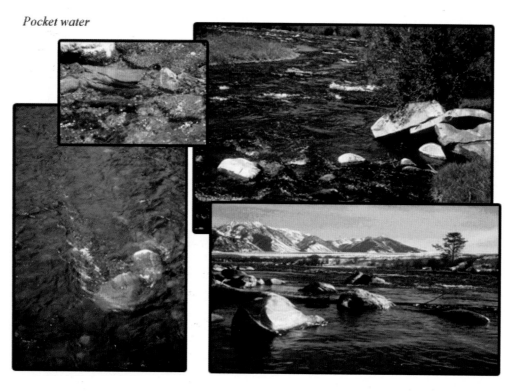

Pocket water

Current seams

Riffles

Fly Fishing: *The Lifetime Sport*　**139**

Foam line

Eddy

Prime lie

Resting lie

Stream characteristics

Dead water

Deep hole

Curvatures

Fallen trees

Fast water

Aquatic weed beds

STILL WATER CHARACTERISTICS

Each lake is unique. Most of a lake's water is barren because its fish seek specific areas to reside. Perhaps only ten percent of a lake has fish, leaving the remainder uninhabited. The following are likely physical structures which attract fish: shallows, weed beds, drop-offs, channels, shoals, cliffs, and inlet/outlet areas. Each will be discussed.

Shallows

A lake's great depths harbor little food or oxygen for fish to exist. A common mistake is to fish a lake's depth instead of its shallows.

A lake's littoral zone is found in water usually less than ten feet deep. This zone provides good growths of submerged aquatic plants. It is here in a lake shallow that adequate amounts of sunlight can penetrate, promoting plant growth and photosynthesis. Also, this littoral zone has the highest concentrations of aquatic insects. In some exceptionally clear lakes, sunlight can penetrate deeper and this littoral zone may be extended to about the thirty foot depth.

The shape of a lake's shoreline influences the characteristics of its shallows. Gentle slopes allow for the accumulation of organic matter while steep slopes do not. Lakes rich in nutrients are classified as atrophic waters while those poor in nutrients are oliotrophic. Nutrients are derived from decomposing bottom materials. This fertilizes both the new plant and insect growths. Irregular shorelines result in more protected bays and areas where decomposing organic matter may collect. A lake's bottom structures may vary widely from mud, gravel, rocky, to weedy areas. It is the weedy areas that are most important for fish life to sustain itself.

The most dominant fish lay claim to the choicest feeding areas. In the shallows fish are vulnerable to birds of prey because they are trapped close to the surface and more visible for these birds. From overhead an osprey may swoop down on a fish and this makes them wary. An angler's stealthy approach is essential for success. The dominant fish seek out areas in the shallows close to nearby channels or drop-offs where they can quickly escape harm.

At times of darkness the shallows are frequented by the most fish. Low lighting shields them from a bird's vision. Hence, fish choose to safely feed in these shallows during dawn/dusk and throughout overcast days. The largest fish rarely expose themselves to direct sunlight in shallow waters.

Weed Beds

The quality of angling and the abundance of aquatic plants are usually directly proportional. Extensive weed beds provide the best fisheries. Henry's Lake, Idaho, is a prime example; in fact, at times in late summer there are so many weeds that trolling is not possible. Yet this lake produces a tremendous number of quality fish.

Nearly all fish food is attracted to weed beds. The rooted submerged plants are the preferred habitat. Also, floating weed beds can be fertile, but the submerged beds are the best homes for the food chain.

As a result fish are found in close proximity to these weeds. The best places to fish are just above submerged plants, adjacent and in between them. Both food and shelter is offered in these places.

Locating submerged plant beds is accomplished by observation from a high vantage point. Looking from a boat or float tube in clear lakes is an alternative when a vantage point is unavailable. Video sonar is of benefit when direct vision is not possible. The water's coloration is a clue in finding weed beds. A light greenish cast as opposed to a deeper blue indicates submerged plants. The juncture of dark blue and light green is an indication of a channel or a drop-off adjacent to the submerged plants. These areas are prime spots for fish.

Shoreline Vegetation

Shorelines with heavy vegetation can be difficult to fish; however, wading or float tubing can provide good access. In addition, shade and cover are provided in these places. A bonus source of terrestrials is included: ants, beetles, hoppers, leaf worms, and caterpillars can be added to the fish's menu. Sometimes these areas are best fished from the lakeside shoreward. Fishing from a silent float tube out in the lake and casting towards the shore is an advantage.

Drop-offs

Fish are driven into the drop-off areas by birds of prey and boat traffic. The drop-offs shelter fish from these annoyances. The deep areas adjacent to the shallows furnish fish easy access to their food supplies. Consequently drop-offs can be highly productive during bright light conditions.

I prefer a sunken retrieve which travels my fly up from the depths along the slope of a drop-off. As the fly travels it becomes more visible to the fish.

In clear water, drop-offs are easily seen by noting the water's color change from deep blue to a lighter green. In stained water, video sonar can help locate the drop-off areas.

Channels

Channels are similar to drop-offs in concentrating fish. These are usually caused by an inlet stream. An added advantage is that some current action may still take place resulting in concentrating food supplies, more oxygen, or better temperature conditions. In times of hot weather channels furnish cooler, more oxygenated water. At these times fish become closely schooled. Channels occur adjacent to a lake shallow and afford protective cover. This depth and protection provides an ideal location for fish to enjoy the incoming food, shade, and at times cooler oxygen enriched water.

Locating channels can be done by visual observation from a high vantage point. Since they can meander in many directions they are hard to find by video sonar alone. It is worth the effort to locate and map the exact locations of channels.

Shoals

Shoals are submerged islands which fail to reach the surface. In deep water areas shoals provide a sudden littoral zone, and aquatic life is attracted to them. Fish have ready access to a drop-off area which surrounds them. Shoals can provide a variety of temperature zones, areas of protection, and additional food supplies.

Utah Lake's Bird Island is an example of a shoal. During high water years it is submerged and hard to locate in this large muddy lake. Bird Island consists of gravel surrounded by vast areas of mud. Outstanding numbers of walleye and catfish live here. Also, Bird Island is a hot spot for duck hunting because its littoral zone provides vegetation which the ducks eat.

Locating shoals is best done by visual observation from a vantage point; again look for lighter greenish areas surrounded by deeper bluish waters. Many times shoals are extensions of land points. A ridge continued out into the lake may contain a shoal. These points can continue out into the water and present a ridge of shallower shoals. Fish are attracted to these ridge points because of their advantageous conditions. Cruising fish must spend more time in these areas traveling a longer distance around such shoals. Look for gravelly points of land extending out into a lake. Video sonar is useful in locating and plotting shoals when direct vision is poor. Map these areas when found because they are consistent fish producers.

Cliffs

Cliffs are great vantage points to look for weed beds, drop-offs, channels, and shoals. Cliffs afford shade, more favorable water temperatures, and collect flotsam which includes drowned or struggling aquatic and terrestrial insects. Some cliffs furnish seepage of spring water which enhances the favorable water temperatures.

Fish occasionally mill about cliff areas, focusing their attention to the surface. Windswept insects may hit the cliff and end up in the water. An errant breeze may blow a terrestrial off a ledge into the water. Commonly, food sources come from the surface in cliff areas so similarly they can be fertile places to fish dry flies.

Cliffs need not be high to be productive. Snowbanks can serve as temporary cliff-like areas. Rocky shorelines are common in both reservoirs and in some natural lakes. These shoreline areas fish well with terrestrials. Drift lines of windblown objects commonly gather at cliffs and rocks.

These rocky shorelines are similar to cliffs. An earth-filled dam provides an ideal rocky shoreline. It is adjacent to a steep drop-off. These drift lines harbor many dead adult and stillborn insects.

Outlets

Outlets gather food like a vacuum pump; consequently both surface and subsurface foods are concentrated by their gradual but increasing current action. Outlets are usually open areas with little hiding places for protection. Fish are wary in these waters and may limit their activities here to times of low light periods.

Yellowstone's Lewis Lake's outlet can produce a few prime fish nearly every time it's fished. Early, late, and during overcast conditions there is a chance there to hook a large brown or lake trout.

I once hooked an enormous wild steelhead in the outlet area of British Columbia's Morice's Lake. In this outlet the fish was holding as if it was in a mariner's tail out. This steelhead was a surprise because at the time I was trout fishing. Respectfully, its first wild run will be long remembered. Every time I visit a lake's outlet I look for a bonus fish opportunity. Using utmost caution I try to make my best approach and presentation.

Inlets

Streams entering a lake provide a food supply and a change in both water temperature and oxygenation. Also, inlet streams concentrate fish at spawning times. In inlet bays fish stack up during the pre-spawn. Inlet areas modify a lake's structure from shallows to increased depths because stream channels erode winding paths through a lake's bottom.

Fish are noticeably alert in these locations because birds of prey have learned that these are good areas to fish.

Incoming current stacks up against the lake's stillwaters to create a mini-rip effect; in fact, these rip currents develop vertical walls of water which concentrate incoming foods. Its surface collection of flotsam is readily noticeable so this concentration of food will attract hungry fish.

Inlet areas are prime locations to fish, especially during low light conditions, warm temperature times, and pre-spawn periods.

Springs

The constant temperature and rich oxygen content of spring water attracts fish in both cold and warm weather times. As a result areas around underwater springs provide prime fishing since they can draw exceptionally large numbers of fish. Springs in conjunction with submerged weed beds are especially productive.

Underwater springs in Henry's Lake are well-known fish producers. They are concealed in areas of submerged weed beds. When the weather is hot, locate an underwater spring and the fish will consistently be there. The difficulty is locating an underwater spring hidden in the midst of such a large expanse of

water. Once found, map its location by triangulation or record it on a GPS. The ability to easily return to underwater springs simplifies fishing. A thermistor on a remote cord is a must in probing a spring's exact location. Fish mill about in incredible numbers simplify fishing because their greed instincts strike up competition for your offering. A variety of flies such as leeches, dragonfly, damselfly, scuds, or a baitfish imitation can be fruitful. Even after spooking the school, resting the area is all that's needed for them to return.

Wind Direction and Drift Lines

Leeward shorelines collect windblown surface debris. In these foam lines are trapped insects and nearby baitfish. Windward shores adjacent to shoreline vegetation can be an additional source of terrestrials. Also, the leeward shore receives a surf action which stirs up the bottom-dwelling aquatic insects and makes them available for predation. Fish may move into the surf to feed. Muddy surf areas are indications that the bottom has been disturbed. Fish the juncture where water clarity improves enough for the fish to readily see your offering. When fishing stained water, slow down your retrieve and make your casts closer together. Make it easy for the fish to find your fly. The muddy surf affords concealment for the foraging fish. A wide variety of fly patterns can be effective because they must only match some of the bottom-dwelling shoreline insects.

Ice Cover

For a short time each spring the shoreline shallows lose their ice lid first while the deeper water is still ice covered. This is a prime time for foraging fish. They are drawn to the ice-free shallows because of warmer temperatures and can cruise the ice shelf juncture in safety. Cast to the ice edge and retrieve parallel to it. The only disadvantage is that this is a short-lived condition. Montana's Hebgen Lake provides exciting action if one casts streamers parallel to its shoreline ice lid. Lunker browns and rainbows charge your flies from underneath the ice cover.

Plant Cover

Lilypad covers are found in the shallows around irregular shorelines. These furnish overhead protective cover for daytime feeding fish. Annoying hangups are common and discourage most anglers, but a weed guard added to your fly can make fishing these places a joy. Cast and carefully retrieve between the pads. Fish use this overhead canopy for protection and prefer these locations. The channels and lilypad edges are good sites for parallel retrieves. Many times a subsurface offering is productive because the fish hold just under the lilypad. Fishing deep in the

midst of the pads is difficult because of all the stems that angle in odd directions. A float tube is helpful because it maneuvers you into a multitude of different casting lanes. The best time to fish lilypad areas is during bright light conditions.

Reservoirs

Reservoirs are man-made lakes constructed by damming up a stream. The flooded canyon or valley provides a widely varied habitat. Engineers design reservoirs to store the greatest amount of water for irrigation, flood control, or electricity production. Hence reservoirs are sited with depths in mind and are usually very deep in character. The dam's height approximates its maximum depth. The significance to the angler is that most of the water of a reservoir lies outside the productive shallow littoral zones. An optimistic angler may view such a reservoir as a place where all of that immense water concentrates its fish in its limited shallows.

New reservoirs are much more productive than old ones. The recent flooding of standing vegetation causes its organic decay to be released into the food chain. This enhanced situation provides a temporary boomtown for aquatic weeds, insects, and fish. After a few years this organic matter is used up and the reservoir loses much of its food chain causing the fishery's decline. Hence, new reservoirs are hot spots which inevitably fade.

A reservoir's terrain conveys much to the structure of its fishery. Flooding vast expanses of shallows can create giant littoral zones. A disadvantage is that these

littoral zones are subject to reservoir draw downs which fluctuate its depths and may cause much of it to go dry during the late summer season. This seasonal fluctuation deteriorates the quality of its littoral zone and of its fishery.

Flood control reservoirs can be subject to much silt being deposited during the runoff times. This can be detrimental to the fishery of such reservoirs. An example is Montana's Ennis Lake which has silted up so severely that it now overheats the water released into the once great Bear Trap Canyon of the Madison River. Now August water temperatures can soar to an excess of 70° F, causing fish kills. This reservoir was initially a great trout producer but has deteriorated into a very limited fishery which has also affected its outlet river.

Utah's enhanced Strawberry/Soldier Creek Reservoir offers a more stable fishery. Here many small streams that are relatively free of silt were damned to form one huge reservoir. Its terrain consists of shallow valleys which when flooded, became immense littoral zones. Its elevation and temperatures are also ideal for trout habitat. Biologists manage this reservoir by stocking and maintaining it as a prime fishery. Strawberry Reservoir is an example of one of the better reservoirs.

The huge Colorado and Green River impoundments had their heydays when they were young. Flaming Gorge Reservoir was a trophy brown and rainbow trout fishery in its early days; now it is primarily a lake trout and smallmouth bass fishery. Lake Powell has changed from a fantastic largemouth bass and crappie fishery to a striped bass one. There are still fish to be caught in these older reservoirs, but it takes some knowledge of where and how to fish them. In their youth, little skill was needed to catch fish.

The key to reservoir fishing is to search out the productive areas such as: inlets, channels, drop-offs, weed beds, shallows, shoals, cliffs, and land points. Using accurate topographic maps of the terrain prior to flooding facilitates the location of these structures. The huge sizes of these reservoirs can easily conceal productive areas. A boat with a quality video sonar and time spent prospecting are assets to productive reservoir fishing.

Large portions of a reservoir harbor few or no fish. All of the fish are found concentrated into the few prime areas. Find these places and spend your time productively fishing them and not wasting your time in the fish-poor areas.

Reservoirs stratify into the epilimnion, thermocline, and hypolimnion areas during the warm months of the year. (See Diagram 1) Since reservoirs tend to be deep, the hypolimnion area can be vast. The epilimnion is where light penetrates causing submerged weed growth. That is the productive portion of a reservoir. It also generates the dissolved oxygen needed to sustain life. The thermocline is the transitional zone with a drastic drop in water temperature which separates the epilimnion and hypolimnion layers. The oxygen and food supply is limited to the epilimnion and somewhat to the thermocline layers. The hypolimnion is usually depleted of food and oxygen making it unproductive. Learn to detect areas where the epilimnion and the thermocline correspond to the lake's bottom. Spend your time fishing these waters and eliminate the hypolimnion area

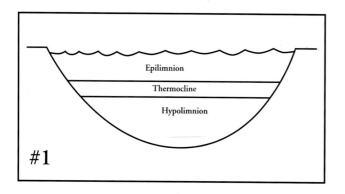

altogether. A thermistor with an oxygen monitor is useful in locating these layers. Next use your video sonar to find structured areas which fall into the desired epilimnion and thermocline areas.

During very warm weather the epilimnion may become too warm to hold adequate oxygen for fish to sustain themselves. Fish will seek the thermocline where cooler waters can hold more oxygen. Remember at this time the hypolimnion is cold but still oxygen poor. The lake's entire fish population can be concentrated into the limited area of the thermocline. Locate bottom structure at the same depth as the thermocline and the fishing can be amazing.

Lake zones are also classified as being littoral, pelagic, and profundal zones; (See Diagram 2) this classification is based on

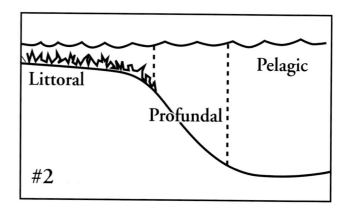

light penetration and plant growth. The littoral zone is where photosynthesis occurs and concentrates the lake's food chain. The profundal zone is the deepest portion of a lake where photosynthesis and plant growth is severely limited; it is where little light penetrates. This profundal zone supports few fish and deep reservoirs harbor vast acreage of this zone. The pelagic zone is the top portion of the profundal zone and this pelagic zone is bordered on its sides by the littoral zones. Penetrating sunlight reaches here and oxygen is high but its bottom is only accessed by going through the dead profundal zone. Its importance is that where the pelagic zone borders with the littoral zone fish can gather. Hiding in this zone, fish venture out into the shallows to ambush prey.

Junctional habitat seems to consistently concentrate animals; big game species such as elk and deer prefer areas adjacent to both open and forested areas. Elk feed in the open park grasses during low light conditions and migrate to hide in the forest cover during the day. Fish likewise use the pelagic zone as a darkened hideaway safe from predators and concealed from their prey. Surprise attacks on schooled minnows are initiated from this pelagic zone. A reservoir's largest fish commonly behave in this manner by ambushing their prey at this littoral/pelagic zone junction.

These three zones of littoral, profundal, and pelagic do not change. It is the epilimnion, thermocline, and hypolimnion layers that are subject to changes due to weather conditions such as temperature changes and wind/wave actions.

When selecting a reservoir to fish, take into account its anatomical features. Choose one with the most fish-producing habitat. Look for one with an abundant littoral zone which has lots of weed beds, shoals, drop-offs, islands, peninsulas, inlets, cliffs, rocky and gravel areas within this zone. Fish these structures adjacent to the pelagic zone which provides both deeper, cooler waters and darkened cover to conceal fish.

When fishing reservoirs with limited littoral zones look for areas with structures located within these zones. The few good areas these reservoirs possess may have been under-fished, so these structured areas may provide a seldom-fished hot spot.

Idaho's failed Teton Dam Reservoir is rarely fished because it was a disaster site. Now its limited backed-up pool contains some of the best trophy cutthroat fishing anywhere. This pool is all prime trout habitat. Every time I've ventured there, I'm alone with its abundant trout and rattlesnakes; it has given up cutthroat weighing as much as nine pounds.

In summary, it is difficult to locate prime fish habitat in reservoirs because the vast amounts of stored water conceal them. Discover a reservoir's features and its fish may be concentrated there. Perhaps you can discover the 10% of a reservoir that holds all of its fish. Identify these places and spend your fishing time angling there.

Natural Lakes

Mother Nature creates natural lakes. Sometimes man enhances them by a strategic placement of a dam. My favorite lakes are natural ones because Mother Nature's design is not hydropower production nor irrigation but aquatic life.

Two of my favorite lakes are Idaho's Henry's Lake and Yellowstone Park's Heart

Lake. These are notable fisheries because their structural elements include vast littoral zones and optimal water quality.

Henry's Lake is all littoral zones with an average depth of about ten feet. Here, great expanses of aquatic plants flourish which produces an enormous food chain. Its trout prosper and their average size is massive. The water's alkalinity is optimal; in addition, its altitude furnishes cool summer waters which allow for long growing seasons.

Heart Lake is a remote lake with similar elements favoring fish production. Here large cutthroat and lake trout are present in prolific numbers. Its forest and water quality is almost untouched by man; a visit to Heart Lake is a superb wilderness experience.

The advantages of a natural lake are that many of them contain large areas of shallows and that their water source comes from underground springs. Here the earth has filtered its water supply and buffered its temperature and chemical contents. Seasonally, snow melt and runoff influences a lake by carrying organic and inorganic matter that can enrich these waters. The best natural lakes have an abundance of littoral zones coupled with good chemistry and water quality. From the weeds in the littoral zone both oxygen and insect habitat are produced.

Usually, natural lakes include deep areas where during severe winter and summer conditions fish can migrate to for survival.

The valuable structures of natural lakes are weed beds, drop-offs, inlet channels and streams, outlet areas, shoals, peninsulas, bays, rock slides, riparian banks, cliffs, and downed timbers. Fish cruise underwater routes in search of emerging insects and other food sources. In the spring, before heavy weed bed growths, the open shallows are prime spots to fish because they warm first. Later in the summer, heavy weed bed growths occur and these shallows may become uncomfortably warm, causing fish to seek nearby cooler channels and drop-offs.

Fishing Strategies

The angling strategy is to start fishing the weed bed areas first because this is the most likely spot to find feeding fish. Take into account the lake's temperature, light intensity, and oxygen content. Next, find where optimal conditions coincide within the weed bed areas. For example, if light intensity is high, fish the darker drop-off areas and channels; likewise, if the water temperature is too warm in the shallows,

seek these same areas. Usually, a lake's highest oxygen concentration will be in the weed bed areas because this is where oxygen is produced by photosynthesis. During low light times, fish are safer to venture out into the shallow, weed bed areas. Fish this water thoroughly, especially the shaded spots adjacent to the weed beds.

During insect emergent times, fish will be drawn to the weed beds to feed; however, at non-emergent times, fish migrate to the nearby safety of the channels and drop-offs. Fishing directly over submerged weed beds is perhaps the most preferred location. Select the optimal sinking line which will suspend your fly just about one foot over these weed beds. Weed guards on fly patterns can be helpful.

Riparian growths, such as reeds and cattails, afford structure that can attract fish. Often, fish hang out just on the edge of these growths. During a damselfly migration the swimming nymphs target these structures for hatching destinations by crawling out of the water onto them to metamorphose. Fish lie in wait to intercept them; also, terrestrial insects inhabit reeds. A wind breeze may topple into the water a grasshopper, ant or a beetle, and fish await these morsels. The transitional waters are the in-between places separating a lake's shallows from its depths. The junction areas where the shallows and the depths meet are prime fishing locations. Here fish migrate to and from each location. Daily movement patterns consist of fish leaving the shallows after the morning feed and again returning to the shallows in

the evening. These transitional areas are the fish's commuting routes. Any bottom structures such as rocks, weeds, or downed trees, enhance transitional waters.

Rocky shorelines are similar to weed beds in growing aquatic insects. A rocky point extending out into the lake provides a structure for fish to cruise around foraging for food. Additionally, baitfish are found in these places and they attract larger predatory fish. Crawfish are common to rocky areas and provide a staple for larger fish. An abrupt rocky shoreline can signify the deepest part of a lake and cooler depths afford a likely fish lie during hot weather conditions.

Cliffs and deep water can occur together as the shoreline cliff extends out into the lake. Additionally, shadows from the cliff furnish cover that attracts fish. These are good places to fish during the heat of the day because these shaded areas contain water that is cooler.

Underwater springs are prominent fishing locations because they are a source of reliable constant temperature and oxygenated water. During both severe hot and cold times fish will seek these springs in astonishing numbers. At these times springs can provide tremendous angling.

Beaver Ponds

Beaver ponds are capable of providing outstanding fishing. They can unexpectedly appear on stretches of small canyon streams that are too small to provide much of a stable fishery. These dams can furnish prime fish habitat where it didn't previously exist. Their locations are sometimes remote and secretive. I have discovered many of my favorite ponds while out in the woods hunting grouse or deer.

The best ponds are located on sections of a spring creek in remote canyon country. The spring creek's rich nutrients and stable temperatures allow for abundant aquatic plant growths. Correspondingly, the insects and trout flourish. This stable oxygen content and favorable temperature prevents them from winterkilling and extends the fish's growing seasons. A beaver dam's main problem is that their engineers must maintain these dams. Beavers can be here today and gone tomorrow. Their dams are temporary structures. Although their

ponds only need a few seasons to quickly become a quality fishery, the beaver may move on before this happens.

A pond built in a freestone creek can provide good fishing, yet they are vulnerable to high run offs which can wash out dams, draining the pond. This makes freestone creek ponds more likely to vanish whereas spring creek ponds are prone to be there for several seasons. The spring creek's advantages of ideal temperatures, stable flows, rich aquatic life, and optimal pH make them the best fishing ponds. Whenever exploring a remote canyon in beaver country, keep an eye out for hidden ponds. I once found several while archery hunting a remote drainage in Utah's Uinta Mountains. A series of about a dozen ponds provided brook trout weighing up to four pounds and cutthroats to three pounds. The fishing was so fantastic that for several years it was the best place I knew to take a beginning flyfisherman. Their first cast would be intercepted by trout swarming the fly from all directions. This fishery lasted for six or seven years yet was eventually abandoned by the beavers and soon deteriorated. I tried to repair one of the failing dams, but I was astounded at the amount of maintenance that they required. Sadly, my efforts were in vain and this great fishery was lost.

Beavers select pond sites adjacent to food supplies such as willow and aspen stands. When hiking in remote canyons where willow or aspen trees grow, search for beaver-chewed trees. Once one is located, you can assume there may be ponds nearby.

When one pond is found, scout out any tributaries nearby in hope of finding more ponds. I usually find them while I'm out hunting when I'm without rod and reel. This happens frequently enough that I now stash in my hunting equipment a tippet spool and a small box of flies. It only takes a minute or two to cut a willow and rig it with a tippet and fly. Seductively dapple a terrestrial fly in the pond to see if it contains fish. If it tests out to be an interesting fishery, return later with your regular tackle.

One advantage of fishing beaver ponds over other lakes is that the fish can be readily caught. Food supplies in beaver ponds are often limited so there is more competition for your fly. Your initial cast may be accosted by several trout with the fastest one being hooked. These trout are usually lightly fished and tend to be naive, foraging type feeders. One downside of good beaver ponds is their remote locations. However, for the serious fly fishermen it's usually well worth the extra effort to hike to a pond filled with naive fish.

Beaver pond country will sometimes result in a surprise sighting of other wildlife such as elk, deer, bear, grouse, coyote, and squirrels. The wildlife adds to the trip. The easily accessed roadside ponds are often discovered early and quickly over fished. The real finds are the unknown remote ones.

Fishing techniques become simplified. You can see, touch, and feel the entire fishery. Overturning stream rocks and vegetation provides you with a grocery list of the fish's foods. Walking around the riparian zone informs you about the local terrestrial insects. It only takes a little investigation to quickly deduce which fly may be the most effective. An exact imitation or a general attractor pattern carefully presented will usually bring an immediate response.

Dry fly fishing is my preferred choice because the beaver pond's surface film is a prime place where most fish feed. After the surface is covered then I probe the channel depths with a sunken fly. I've found leeches, small streamers, nymphs, sculpins, and scud patterns seductively retrieved through the old stream channel to be highly effective. Both slow hand twist and quick strip retrieves are good choices. Fish the pond's deeper waters after you have caught a few on the surface as the frightened fish will seek shelter in these depths.

Tackle requirements are modest. This is a place for an ultra-light outfit. Two and three weight rods, reels and lines are prime choices for these fisheries. Flies are simple assortments of dries, nymphs, streamers, and terrestrials. A floating line and finely tapered leader completes your tackle. Your boxes should easily fit into a jacket pocket and waders are substituted for hiking shoes, although in some wet areas ultra-light waders may be necessary to allow you complete access to the pond's features.

Selecting Alpine Lakes

When I was young I loved to fish alpine lakes. The scenic perfection of Utah's High Uinta lakes drew my attention. I learned early that a lake's remoteness equated into great fishing; consequently, an arduous hike led to an angling treasure.

In the sixties I explored hundreds of back country lakes in search of the perfect Shangri-la. I hoped that my next trek would lead to a paradise with huge trout and outstanding scenery. My Shangri-la was never found, but I did experience some great fly fishing.

Then the seventies came and with it an explosion in outdoor recreation. Back-packing became popular and equipment technology boomed; thus, my once remote lake basins were filled with backpackers. Soon the fishing demised. It even became difficult to find firewood at some of my old favorite lakes. I lost interest in the high lakes and spent my time fishing the valley waters.

Nowadays an emphasis on catch and release has somewhat restored the fisheries. The pristine surroundings and the strikingly beautiful trout make alpine lake fishing a

splendid experience although the rules have changed. Remoteness no longer equates to excellent fishing--it is the least visited lakes that afford the best angling.

Search for the overlooked lakes with faint trails leading to them. For example, I found a small isolated lake sitting just a half mile from the major trail. It provided excellent angling.

Alpine lakes are usually glacier-cut depressions found in mountainous cirques; they collect the ground water and the snow melt. Western alpine lakes usually are sited at high altitudes exceeding 9,000 feet. The summer growing season can be a brief one running from July through mid-September. Because of these elevations, winter snows can occur any time in September. This brief season affords marginal time for fish growth, but a lake's isolation safeguards them for maximum fish growth.

Some alpine lakes are fruitful while others are not. In general, alpine lakes are less fertile than their valley counterparts. Aquatic weed growths are marginal and insect density is sparse. This limited environment is not conducive to abundant fish production; nevertheless, choose the lakes that are seldom used for they provide the best fishing.

Complications from winterkill devastate many alpine lakes. Here a combination of thick ice cover and heavy snow cover shield the available sunlight. Plant growth and photosynthesized oxygen are stopped and decomposing aquatic plants use up the limited oxygen supply. Since the lake is sealed by an ice layer, oxygen from the air is unavailable. Dissolved oxygen levels drop causing the fish to die.

Winterkill occurs most often in lakes which are sheltered from the winter winds. It is these lakes that accumulate the most snowpack. In contrast, the wind swept lakes are scoured from heavy snowfall accumulations. Therefore these lakes

receive more penetrating light. Light is necessary for plants to produce oxygen.

Lakes under the shadow and protection of north slopes receive less wind and more snowpack resulting in a potential winter-kill. Likewise, lakes enjoying a southern exposure receive more sunlight and wind. For example, wintering elk herds collect on the high windswept areas where the grasses are uncovered. Adjacent areas receive the same snowfall amounts but the winds distribute the snow unequally. Heavy drifts occur alongside the windswept shallow collections. Avoid the unlucky lakes sited in areas where the deepest snows collect. Some other factors such as the presence of subsurface springs and optimal depths can deter winterkill.

Seasonal snowfall variances affect the lakes subject to winterkill. A mild winter will prevent one.

When scouting alpine lakes, select the ones that are protected from heavy snowdrifts. Choose the southern exposure lakes because they are more likely to receive more sunlight and less snowpack.

Alpine lakes are similar to their valley counterparts in that they share the same structural features, but a primary difference is that alpine lakes usually have lower oxygen levels than lower altitude lakes. This is especially prevalent in the lakes' deepest hypolimnion zones. During late summer, trout must migrate away from the depths and concentrate in the shallows where oxygen is produced by aquatic plants. In late season avoid the lakes' depths and fish the shallows.

In addition, fish in high lakes must spend more time foraging for a wide assortment

most surface materials will be blown to and collected here as flotsam in drift lines so fish will migrate to feed upon this collection of insects. Additionally, the waves will dislodge aquatic insects from weed beds and rock gardens. These insects become readily available to feeding fish. Casting into surf with nymph patterns can be highly productive. For example, Yellowstone Lake's surf collects an abundance of feeding fish that can be spotted in the waves. These concentrated fish can be easily reached with a short cast.

I love to visit lakes that I have not yet fished. With thousands of lakes to choose

of foods because the insect hatches can be sporadic and meager. Other aquatic foods such as terrestrials, water boatmen, scuds, and leeches are readily ingested. In fact, alpine fish are not as selective as their valley counterparts.

The wind plays an important role in fishing lakes. The windward shore is found on the lakeside that the wind is blowing from; therefore, terrestrial insects are blown off shoreline perches. Look for fish feeding upon ants, beetles, spruce moths, grasshoppers, houseflies, spiders, and the like. Fish terrestrial fly patterns along these windward shorelines.

On the opposite side of the lake lies the wave-beaten shoreline. Eventually

from perhaps my lost Shangri-la still exists.

Fishing pressure is an essential factor in determining productivity. Since these lakes are small and have brief growing seasons, man's use can greatly influence them. The limited fish population can be decimated by just a few anglers. Always exercise conservation by limiting your take to what you can really use. Look for alpine lake basins with an abundance of wildlife. Areas with large elk herds have limited human usage so you may find excellent fishing. An abundance of shy wildlife is a good indicator of a lake's fishing potential.

Another method of locating seldom visited lakes is to use a compass to mark on a map a three mile radius scribe line along all access roads and trails. Next, explore the areas outside of the scribe lines. Most human activity occurs within three miles of trails and roads.

Let me share with you a treasure of an alpine lake which is remotely sited in Utah's Boulder Mountains. This little traveled hike is through both a heavy downfallen forest and a huge lava field. The spring pond sits hidden below a caldera. The area shows no signs of man's usage but is frequented by a shy cinnamon black bear. The fishing rivals northern Canada with willing brook trout exceeding four pounds. A day spent here is like a journey back into pioneer times.

Still Water Exposure

Terrestrial insects thrive in the shoreline vegetation.

Grassy banks harbor foraging fish.

Shoreline vegetation furnishes both shade and cover.

Submerged plants furnish prime habitat.

Islands and shoals provide added littoral zones.

Drop-offs shelter fish from bird predation.

A lake's depths can be void of fish life.

Springs furnish constant temperatures and oxygen.

Wind drift collects insects in foam lines.

Land points concentrate foraging fish.

Outlets concentrate food.

Inlets erode winding channels through a lake bottom.

Inlets can provide spawning habitat.

Streams entering a lake provide a change in both temperature and oxygen.

Lake fish are heavier than stream fish.

Lake Characteristics

Downed trees provide structure for fish to hide.

Fish cruise the ice shelf in safety.

Cliffs gather windblown foods.

Shallows

Aquatic vegetation grows insects.

Lilypads provide cover for daytime feeding fish.

Shallows provide both food and oxygen.

Lake Exposure

Alpine lake

Natural lake

Beaver pond

AQUATIC 9 ENVIRONMENT

The aquatic environment's components which relate to the fish are aquatic plants, temperature, light, oxygen, pH, and the surface film. Each will be discussed so that the angler has a better understanding of the factors that influence a fish's behavior.

Aquatic Plants

The presence of aquatic plants is one of the best indicators of whether a lake or a stream will be a good producer of fish. Most aquatic life which fish feed upon requires these plants for food. Plants also provide a fishery with protective cover and life-giving oxygen.

Aquatic plants are classified into submerged, floating, and emergent varieties.

Submerged plants are rooted on the water's bottom but do not extend all the way to its surface. Eelgrass is an example

of a submerged plant. Floating plants are not rooted and are free to move about the water's surface. Duckweed is an example of a floating plant. Emergent plants are rooted on the water's bottom and extend to its surface. The waterlily is an example of an emergent plant.

The most important plant class is the submerged variety because it provides an abundance of aquatic food on the lake's or stream's bottom. It is also easier to fish than the other two because it produces less plant clutter and snags.

Plants require sunlight for growth and photosynthesis to occur. Plants are restricted to waters receiving sunlight. In most waters, a depth of ten to thirty feet is the limit that sunlight can penetrate. This means that plants are most abundant in the shallows and decrease in quantity as the water deepens. Shallow shorelines protected from floods and wave actions favor the most abundant growths.

In general there are three zones of aquatic plants. (See Diagram 1) The first zone consists mainly of rooted plants with their tops extended to the surface air. These consist of emergent plants. They occur in depths from the edge of shorelines to about the six foot depth. Cattails, reeds, and others are common plants found in this first zone.

The second zone is made up of rooted plants which shelter floating portions on the surface. This zone is deeper than the first zone and spreads to about the ten foot depth. Waterlilies and pond weeds are examples.

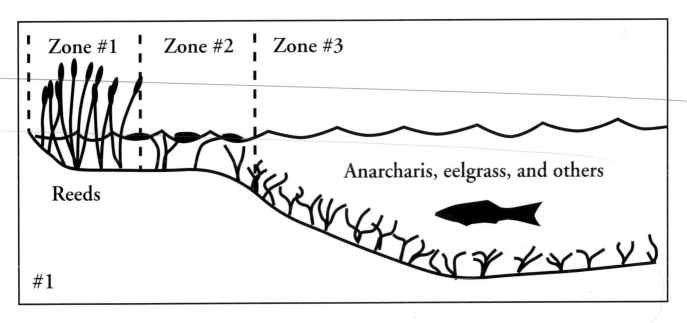

Zone #1　　Zone #2　　Zone #3

Reeds

Anarcharis, eelgrass, and others

#1

The third zone lies in the deeper areas beyond the first two zones. It includes submerged plants such as eelgrass, Anarchasis and others. This zone advances close to a ten foot depth. In very deep, clear waters where sunlight can penetrate deeper, this zone may extend to about the thirty foot depth. Large dense growths of submerged plants are frequented by feeding fish. Submerged plants in the deeper areas are difficult to see and to determine their presence.

These three zones somewhat overlap. In areas of heavy currents, flood and wave action can dismantle plant growth and in some of these areas plants may be absent.

The most desirable plants to locate are the submerged growths of zone three. These support adequate depth for protective cover and an ample food supply.

Specific plants are favored by different aquatic life forms. Callibaetis mayflies, dragonflies, and damselflies are found in certain plants such as the submerged varieties. These insects are stalkers and lie in wait to prey upon their victims.

Fish forage the aquatic plants looking for food. It is these plants that generate most of the fish's food supply.

Light

Light influences fish's activities. A photoperiod is defined as the amount of daylight in a twenty four hour period. It is influenced by the amount of cloud cover on a daily basis. Seasonally, summer months have longer photoperiod days and the sunlight's angle is more direct. The fall, winter, and spring months include both shorter daylight periods and lowered sunlight angulations. In addition, there are longer shadows than during the mid-summer times. Seasonal variances influence the amount of light entering the water.

Fish are more alert during bright sunlight conditions because they are more visible to animals of prey. The fish's food supplies are most abundant in the shallow littoral zones which are located in areas of more intense light penetration necessary for

photosynthesis. Fish may only feel safe to be in these shallow zones during subdued lighting conditions. This is usually early and late in the day or at times of seasonal low light conditions which occur in the fall, winter, and spring. During mid-summer, a fish's presence in the shallows may be restricted to times of dawn, dusk, or overcast days. Consequently fish collect during bright light conditions into the darker areas adjacent to the littoral zones.

With present lighting conditions taken into consideration, select your fishing site accordingly. During the winter, spring, and fall, you will most likely find fish spending more time in the shallows than they do during the summer season. Dark, overcast, and rainy days can draw an abundance of fish into the shallows to feed. Dusk and dawn are also prime times for fishing these shallows. As the light intensity increases, the fish converge into the darker depths of adjacent channels and drop-offs.

Light affects insect's activities. Usually they are most dynamic during low light periods. During intense lighting periods insects search out shaded areas deep in protective cover. The evening rise happens

as insects lay their eggs upon the surface at dusk. Overcast days prolong surface feeding because both the insects are more active and the fish are safer feeding in the shallows. With little knowledge of optical physics, the seasonal and dusk/dawn light phenomenon can be explained. Light rays striking the water's surface at a right angle travel through it with little deviation.

The angulated sunlight is less illuminating underwater because some of it is reflected away at the surface as rays hitting the water are bent upwards; thus the net result is diminished light penetrating the aquatic environment.

There are other light physics phenomena such as infrared rays which are elongated and penetrate cloud cover more readily. This red light from the visible spectrum is noticed more by the fish. Adding the color red to a fly improves its effectiveness, especially in baitfish imitations. Red is more visible.

In conclusion, lighting affects both the insect's and the fish's activities; it's an important factor in finding actively feeding fish.

Oxygen

Oxygen is essential to all aquatic animal life. Without it respiration is impossible. Because the distribution of oxygen throughout a body of water can vary widely, it is important to find the specific areas which hold optimal amounts to support fish life. Oxygen concentration is a prime factor in locating where specific fish species are found.

It's self-evident that air includes an abundance of oxygen; however, water holds a much smaller amount. For example, one liter of air contains about 210 cubic centimeters of oxygen while one liter of water has only about 9 cubic centimeters. In air the lack of oxygen is rarely a problem, but in water its effect is more apparent. Water harbors a tenuous margin of safety because its oxygen content is small and varies widely. Insufficient oxygen supplies will result in animal death.

Two physical factors affecting water's oxygen content are altitude (atmospheric pressure) and temperature. Oxygen solubility in water increases with decreases in both temperature and altitude. Conversely, oxygen solubility decreases with rises in temperature and altitude.

Atmospheric pressure is inversely proportional to altitude. That is, a rise in altitude lowers the atmospheric pressure, and a decrease in altitude raises the atmospheric pressure. On the other hand, atmospheric pressure is directly proportional to oxygen water solubility. That is, a rise in atmospheric pressure increases the water's oxygen content while a decrease in atmospheric pressure lowers the water's oxygen content.

Oxygen diffusion occurs at the water's surface, and its mixing throughout happens during a lake's spring and fall turnover times. The oxygen diffusion process is very slow. Both wind and wave actions mix oxygen at the surface, while plant photosynthesis generates oxygen when plants are present. In deep water, where light cannot penetrate, oxygen cannot be produced by plants. Hence, a lake's hypolimnion only receives its limited oxygen by spring and fall mixing turnovers. This is why a lake's greatest depths can become so oxygen poor. The stratification of water layers seals the hypolimnion from the surface air supply and this seal is only interrupted at spring and fall.

An increase in water temperature lowers the amount of oxygen it can contain. During hot conditions a lake's shallows may become too warm to hold sufficient oxygen, and the animal life forms must migrate to cooler regions which have more oxygen. Inlet streams and underwater springs can supply the needed oxygenated

water. The deeper shaded areas just above the thermocline can be cool enough to hold sufficient oxygen. Fish concentrate in these limited areas when such conditions prevail.

Since a lake depends upon wave action, photosynthesis, and currents to mix and produce its oxygen, areas of adequate and inadequate oxygenated water exist simultaneously. This results in areas where fish can and cannot live. It is a precarious balancing act which includes oxygen content, temperature, light intensity, protective cover, and available food supply that dictates just where fish can be found.

The altitude's influence on an alpine lake can be dramatic. For example, in my youth I spent considerable time fishing alpine lakes above ten thousand feet in altitude. During the dog days of summer my success dramatically fell. I was puzzled because these alpine lakes contained colder water than their valley counterparts. The alpine lakes' depths were void of fish, and my success was limited to the lakes' shallows. Earlier in the season the angling was good in the alpine lakes' depths. Now in midsummer the fishing was poor. The valley lakes fished best in their depths while the alpine lakes fished best in their shallows. I neglected to take into account the difference in altitude and atmospheric pressure between the alpine and valley lakes. The high altitude lakes' oxygen was less because there was less oxygen available when the spring and fall turnovers occurred. This limited oxygen supply was quickly depleted in the alpine lakes' depths, making it so fish couldn't live there. The lower elevation lakes took in higher oxygen content during the spring and fall turnover times. This confined the alpine lakes' fish to the shallows while the valley lakes' fish were in the lakes' depths. I once thought that all big fish lived in the depths and only small ones were in the shallows. This notion is untrue.

The current in a river mixes oxygen much better than limited currents and waves in a lake. Also, this thorough mixing causes little variation in both, oxygen and temperature differences. During high temperature times, the whitewater river sections mix higher oxygen content. In times of hot spells fish may migrate to the rapids for survival.

Look for them in the pocket areas downstream from rapids. Also areas close to adjacent inlet streams and underwater springs can harbor more favorable conditions. For example, in warm thermal rivers such as Yellowstone Park's Firehole River, fish migrate to the mouths of cooler tributary streams during warm seasons.

In conclusion, the oxygen content of water is a prime factor in determining the location of fish. An adequate oxygen supply is essential to sustain fish life.

PH

The pH scale is a measure of the acid and base concentration of a solution. A pH of 7 is neutral; 0-7 is the acid range and 7-14 is the base or alkalinity range.

The presence of dissolved carbonates, bicarbonates, and hydroxides in water is associated with alkalinity. The presence of dissolved organic matter in water causes it to be more acidic in nature.

Fast growing fish are associated with alkaline waters; whereas slow growing fish are associated with acidic waters. Alkaline waters enhance the amount of aquatic foods

and weed beds. On the other hand, acidic waters curtail this production of aquatic foods and weed beds.

Acid rain can cause water to become too acidic for life, causing both fish and insect kills. A spring snowmelt can concentrate the acid in the bottom layer of the snowbank. When this last layer melts, high concentrations of acids are released into the watershed. This can be disastrous to aquatic life.

Local areas of a lake can vary in pH. Serious bass fishermen frequently measure the water's pH to determine where bass may be concentrated.

In general, I avoid the acidic lakes and streams in favor of the alkaline ones. Perhaps this explains why so many Pacific Northwest waters are poor producers of non-anadromous fish. They are nearly barren of aquatic insect life. The abundant rainfall is so intense that these waters become soft and acidic, and the carbonates and alkaline elements have been depleted. The organic matter has concentrated in them. High desert waters favor alkalinity because less rainfall does not wash away the alkaline elements. Their weed bed growth and abundant insect life provide more ideal conditions for fast growing fish. I'm always amazed that a desert state like Nevada has such productive water while the rain forest of the Oregon Coast has an abundance of waters that are nearly void of residential fish. If it weren't for anadromous fish, many coastal streams would not have fish.

Surface Film

Surface film tension is the property of a liquid by which it acts as if its surface is a stretched elastic membrane. This tension allows insects to stand on the water's surface. Surface film tension is caused by the attraction of water molecules to each other; in addition, the surface molecules are attracted to the underlying molecules.

The amount of surface film tension is affected by both temperature and dissolved substances. An increase in temperature lowers the net force of attraction among molecules and so decreases the surface tension. An increase in dissolved organic substances also lowers the surface tension. However, an increase in dissolved inorganic salts causes a rise in surface tension. So if you want to try to walk on water, do so on a cold day in a salty lake.

Surface film tension is the property which allows items that are not wetted to float. It is also the reason why floatant is placed on our lines and flies to prevent these objects from being wetted. They will float on the surface film.

The surface film also reflects light; similarly, it reduces the amount of light entering the water. This influences both the angler's and the fish's vision.

Emerging aquatic insects must be able to break through this surface tension to reach the air. At times, when this surface tension is great, insects have difficulty emerging through the surface. They may become trapped in the surface film and vulnerable to fish predation. The cooler, overcast days provide a longer surface duration of insects hatching because they have more difficulty piercing the surface film. Being trapped at the surface, insects are forced to drift for a prolonged time.

Surface tension commonly traps terrestrial insects which fall into the water. An increase in surface tension makes it more difficult for these terrestrial insects to escape.

Hence cooler temperatures enhance the angling production during emergences of midge, mayfly, and caddisflies by prolonging the insect's presence at the surface.

A fresh rain may cause an increase in dissolved organic or inorganic substances in the water. If it's an increase in inorganic salts, the surface tension rises; on the other hand, if it's an increase in organic substances, the surface tension lowers.

Warm temperatures favor the insect's escape by lowering the surface tension. During warmer temperatures, hatching insects are not on the surface for long. During extremely high surface tension

times heavy objects such as snails may be found floating.

Best dry fly conditions are when the surface film tension is high. The trapped insects are prolonged at the surface and this elicits fish predation.

Temperature

The purpose of this writing is to provide background information concerning the relationship between water temperature and fish. Since fish inhabit only a small fraction of a body of water, it is imperative to be able to locate these areas; otherwise, it is a waste of your time to fish in areas void of fish. Knowledge of temperature's influence on fish can help you both locate and catch them.

Background Data

Fish are coldblooded animals with their body temperatures controlled by their environments. Temperature directly affects their activities, and each fish species has an ideal temperature range in which they are the most active. Since fish can detect changes as slight as 0.1° F, a small change in temperature does not go unnoticed.

Likewise, aquatic insects are cold blooded creatures. Temperature influences insects' activities such as emergence and migration. Because aquatic insects are a fish's primary food source, their availability directly influences the fish's feeding activities. A water's greatest thermal source is solar radiation which is directly absorbed. The surrounding air mass likewise affects water's temperature by conduction at the surface. Heat is also transferred from the water's bottom sediments and adjacent rocky shorelines. This last source has only a minor influence on water temperature; the first two factors play primary roles.

Water loses heat from evaporation, outlet flows, and air conduction. Wind action distributes heat in a body of water by causing waves which mix the water.

A large water mass is slow to change temperature as it is efficient at holding its energy. Consequently, large lakes are slow to warm up in the spring; likewise, they are slow to cool down in the fall. It requires a tremendous amount of energy measured in kilocalories to influence a temperature change in a large body of water. This is why water temperatures always lag behind the air temperature changes.

Lakes stratify or divide into three layers defined by both temperature and oxygen content. The water's oxygen content and temperature are inversely proportionate. That is the cooler the water the more oxygen it will hold; conversely, the warmer the water the less oxygen it will hold. In general, water is at its greatest weight density when it is at 39.2° F. As a result, the deepest water will be the densest and closest to this 39.2° F. As water warms it becomes proportionally less dense and stratifies towards the surface. Water cooler than 39.2° F also becomes less dense and will be found at the surface. Water's melting/freezing point is at about 32° F and this is found at the surface because it is less dense than the 39.2° F water. Ice is a solid phase which due to its crystalline structure is even less dense than its liquid phase. That is why ice develops on a lake's surface.

During warm weather times, a lake stratifies into epilimnion, thermocline, and hypolimnion layers. (See Diagram 1)

The epilimnion is the uppermost layer which is both well oxygenated and uniform in temperature. The thermocline is a mid layer containing a drastic temperature reduction and decreased oxygen content. The hypolimnion is the bottom layer characterized by both the lowest oxygen content and the coldest water approaching 39.2° F. These bottom two layers are oxygen poor because they are remote from the oxygen producing surface and aquatic plant areas. These layer's increased densities cause a barrier which seals them from obtaining additional oxygen supplies.

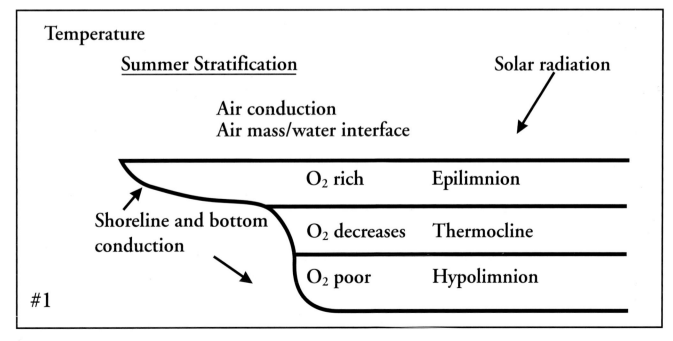

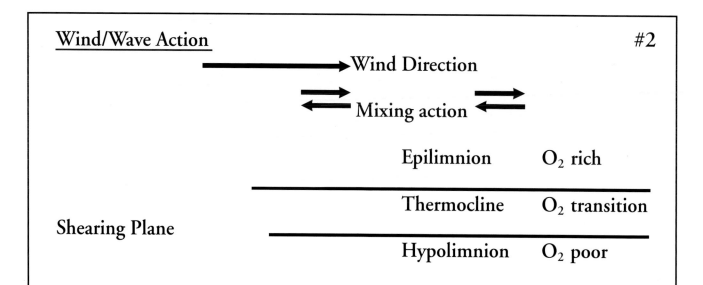

Wind/Wave Action #2

Wind Direction

Mixing action

Shearing Plane

Epilimnion   O₂ rich

Thermocline   O₂ transition

Hypolimnion   O₂ poor

Wind/Wave action mixes the lake's epilimnion layer. Extreme winds can mix thermocline and hypolimnion layers. As water cools in the fall the colder more dense surface water sinks down through thermocline and hypolimnion causing the layers to mix.

As a result, thermocline and hypolimnion layers are oxygen poor.

In the fall as water temperatures approach 32° F throughout, the lake mixes and these stratification layers are lost. (See figure 2) At this time all of the lake's water reaches the same temperature and density. This blending distributes the oxygen evenly throughout the lake. Wind and wave action also help the mixing. After ice out in the spring, this wave action again mixes the water and causes the loss of winter thermal stratification. These periods are often referred to as spring and fall turnover times. Since the turnover mixes the oxygen evenly, fish can be found scattered throughout a lake. During summer and winter stratification times, fish can only live in restricted areas where oxygen is plentiful and temperature is comfortable. Winter conditions cause the coldest 32° F water to

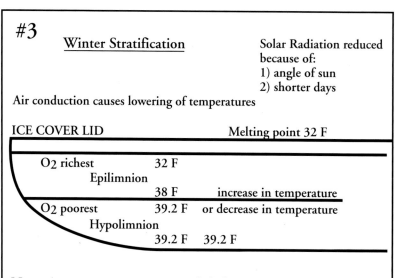

#3   Winter Stratification

Solar Radiation reduced because of:
1) angle of sun
2) shorter days

Air conduction causes lowering of temperatures

ICE COVER LID   Melting point 32 F

O₂ richest   32 F
        Epilimnion
                        38 F   increase in temperature
O₂ poorest   39.2 F   or decrease in temperature
        Hypolimnion
                        39.2 F   39.2 F

Note: As water temperature cools below 39.2 F it buoys upwards cooling the water masses above. During extreme cold the warmest water at 39.2 F will sink to the bottom with the cooler water rising above with 32 F freezing at the surface

be on the surface and the warmest 39.2° F water to be on the lake's bottom. (See Diagram 3) A lake's ice lid cover in winter prohibits mixing by wind/wave action and locks in the stratification layers. Under the ice, oxygen production comes from photosynthesis caused by light penetration reaching the aquatic plants. A heavy snow and ice cover shields this needed light penetration and curtails oxygen production by plant photosynthesis.

During the winter the top hypolimnion water layer has the most oxygen, aquatic life, and fish. The middle thermocline layer is absent. The bottom hypolimnion layer is oxygen poor and devoid of life. Winter fish kill is caused by a complete blocking of sunlight penetration causing the aquatic plants to die. (See Diagram 4) The decaying of dead plants uses oxygen and depletes the lake's oxygen causing fish death from suffocation. Aquatic animals further deplete oxygen by respiration.

During hot weather, fish are found close to the bottom layer of the epilimnion. They opt for the coolness of the thermocline but still require the oxygen richness of the epilimnion. Commonly, fish daily migrate to the shallows to feed and return to the comfort of the epilimnion-thermocline junction. Resting fish are most comfortable at this junction.

During the fall turnover, a lake blends these three layers into one uniform body of water with stable oxygen and temperatures throughout. This causes the fish to become highly active and very hungry. In the fall fish can become scattered due to these widespread ideal conditions.

Water temperatures initiate insect hatches. A cooler than normal year delays seasonal insect migrations. The calendar timing of an insect hatch can be altered by variations in local temperatures. For example, a cold front can delay the stonefly hatch on a river, spoiling a planned vacation. In addition, unseasonably warm temperatures may cause this same hatch to occur earlier than usual. Aquatic insects demand well-oxygenated water for emergence. Unseasonably warm temperatures may deplete the water's oxygen content and retard insect emergence.

A stream's current thoroughly blends its water, resulting in fairly uniform temperature and oxygen contents, but small

---

#4

Heavy snow cover   Thick ice lid

O_2 poor throughout

Decaying plants
(deplete O_2)

temperature variations may still happen. Since fish can detect a 0.1° F difference, they may seek out more favorable water temperatures during extreme warm weather conditions. At these times fish search out submerged springs and some cooler tributaries. For example, during extremely warm weather in Yellowstone Park, the Firehole River's trout will school below the confluence of cooler tributary streams.

I believe that fish become activated by a sudden swing in temperature which brings the water to the fish's ideal range. Especially after a prolonged spell of unfavorable warm or cold temperatures, this sudden change toward ideal temperatures highly activates the fish. This results in the fish going on a sudden active feeding spree. For example, a February Chinook-wind provokes a water temperature swing from stable thirties to the mid-forties° F. The fish answer by going on a feeding frenzy. The peculiarity of this event is that the forty degree temperatures are far below the trout's preferred range of 55-60° F. The trout behave like college students from Minnesota on spring break in Texas. Likewise, if the dog days of summer are cooled by a sudden storm front causing a favorable cooler temperature swing, again the fish respond by actively feeding.

Two conditions resulting in extremely inactive fish are extreme cold (melting point) and heat (greater than 70° F for trout). During these times fish are so inactive it is as if they have disappeared. Perhaps they have migrated elsewhere.

During hot temperature times fly fishermen must monitor the water temperature to find the depth of the epilimnion/thermocline junction. (See Diagram 5) During high light conditions, target fish in the deepest portion of the epilimnion layer because the fish will concentrate there to rest. During low light conditions fish the upper layers of the epilimnion because fish migrate there to

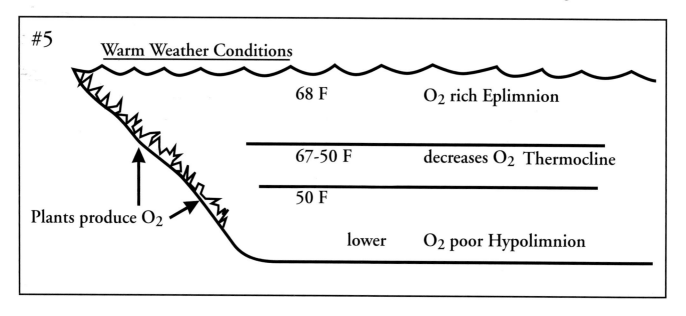

#5   Warm Weather Conditions

68 F   O$_2$ rich Eplimnion

67-50 F   decreases O$_2$ Thermocline

50 F

Plants produce O$_2$

lower   O$_2$ poor Hypolimnion

feed. In both cases locate areas where these depths coincide with bottom structures such as submerged weed beds.

In warm weather fish are most likely found at the junction of the epilimnion and the thermocline. The best area to locate fish is where this junction meets bottom structures such as submerged weed beds, shoals, and rocky bottoms. During these warm conditions fish will be concentrated in these areas during times of bright sunshine. At low light times they migrate to the shallows for feeding. Other fish species will behave similarly except their ideal temperature range will be different. For example, largemouth bass prefer 68-78° F and would be located just under the water surface. Look for protective cover structure just under the surface to find bass.

Using Water Temperature in Locating Fish

The angler should know how to locate fish by temperature. Probe a lake's depth with a thermistor on a calibrated cord. The thermistor registers instant temperatures and the cord marks the depth. I have used a Depth-O-Therm instrument for years. There are newer models out which also register oxygen content, pH, and water clarity. These instruments are useful lake fishing tools. With whatever instrument you select, document the temperature at one foot intervals from the lake's top to its bottom. You rarely need to go deeper than forty feet because it's rare to find fertile water deeper than this depth. Simply find the depth corresponding to the preferred temperature range of the fish species you are seeking. Then identify the ideal temperature depth which coincides with the lake's bottom structures that produce both food and cover. This is a likely spot to find actively foraging fish.

Other factors such as light intensity, water clarity, pH, and oxygen content influence the fish by forcing them to migrate where these factors are favorable.

During hot temperatures when the epilimnion layer is unfavorably warm, find the junction of the epilimnion and thermocline. At this juncture the most oxygen and somewhat cooler temperatures will be found. Target this junction at depths corresponding with bottom structures presenting both food and cover. At these times all of the lake's fish may be concentrated into this narrow zone.

Species	Preferred Temperatures	Species	Preferred Temperatures
Brown Trout	60-65 F	Northern Pike	60-70 F
Lake Trout	48-52 F	Walleye	65-70 F
Rainbow Trout	55-60 F	Yellow Perch	65-72 F
Chinook Salmon	48-55 F	Striped Bass	60-70 F
Coho Salmon	48-55 F	White Bass	65-75 F
Largemouth Bass	68-78 F	Bluegill	75-80 F
Smallmouth Bass	67-71 F	Crappie	70-75 F

Since a stream's current thoroughtly mixes its contents, a single thermometer recording at one location will suffice. The closer this temperature is to the fish's ideal range, the more active the fish will behave. This activity level determines how aggressively fish will feed. For instance, during extreme cold, fish forage in narrow feeding lanes close to their resting lies. On the other hand, ideal temperatures activate fish into chasing food all over the place including the surface film. During ideal temperatures, fish will be attracted to the feeding areas and away from the resting lies. So temperature influences the angler's fly selection, size, presentation and retrieve.

WADING 10

The basic wading rule is to have one foot secured at all times. Never attempt another step without one foot affixed to the bottom. Spills happen when this basic rule is broken. Slow down your wading pace to make sure at all times that one of your feet is anchored. In order to safely wade, first move one foot and secure it; next, maneuver your other foot and also secure it.

The force of the current can be lessened by decreasing your surface area exposed to the current by placing both legs side by side against the flow. (See Diagram 1)

When probing for your next step, do not maneuver your secured foot until your probing foot is anchored. In wading across stream, the current's force is lessened by wading diagonally downstream. In contrast the current's force is enhanced by wading in an upstream direction.

WADING EQUIPMENT
Felt Soles

Felt soles provide traction on slippery, moss covered rock. Consequently felt soles are a good choice for wading rocky streams. But felts can furnish poor footing on inclined muddy banks where they can slide downhill like skis. In muddy areas watch your step when wearing felt soles. Cleated rubber soles provide good footing in muddy areas. The deeper the tread the better they perform in the mud. Rubber cleats are useful in some streams where recently flooded gravel has not yet formed moss coverings.

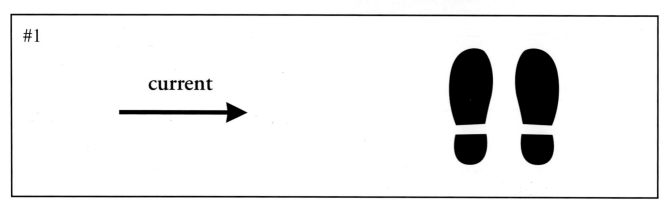

#1

current

Once vegetation has attached to the stream's stones, rubber cleats are poor choices because they provide slippery footing.

Aluminum studs and cleats cut through the moss slime and grip the stone's surface. They provide stable footing on slippery, rocky streambeds. The disadvantages are that they are abrasive to boat bottoms, car floors and fly lines. They can be noisy when used in an aluminum boat or when wading in a rocky streambed. These noises may frighten fish.

Combination felt and aluminum cleats provide the most stable footing on the slickest rocks. But their weight may cause loss of buoyancy during an accidental spill that turns into a swim. Also they are abrasive and noisy, but they do provide the best all-around footing.

Staff

A staff allows a third point to apply stabilizing pressure during a wade. Staffs are useful in difficult wading conditions; also, staffs can be used as probes to feel out your next footing site. When deep wading, place the staff upstream from your upstream foot and apply pressure to secure it to the bottom. Next, move your foot downstream to the new position. Always leave one foot secured. This combination of at least one secure foot and a stable staff position enhances your wading stability.

Use a lanyard to attach the staff onto your wading belt. When it is not in use, allow the staff to hang downstream out of the way. In addition, this staff can be used as a hiking aide. Moreover, it can be used to forewarn snakes by tapping it ahead of your progress.

Staffs can be made streamside by attaching an extra boot lace to an appropriately sized tree limb. Folding staffs are available with shock cording so they assemble by themselves when unsheathed. In addition, staffs can be made from ski poles with the snow loop removed.

Additional Wading Principles

The deeper you wade the less secure your footing becomes because the water's displacement buoys you upwards so that your effective weight is lessened. The current's flow affects you more as you wade deeper because it pushes on a larger surface area of yourself that is underwater. This along with the buoying effect will reach a point where you cannot securely stand in the flow. In addition, the faster the current the more water pressure is exerted upon you.

Use good judgment when evaluating the current speed and depth. Select appropriate footwear and use a staff to secure your footing. In case of a spill, do not panic! Exercise common sense by aiming your feet downstream with your head upstream and simply ride it out. Sooner or later you will likely be swept to a safe exiting place. Lying on your back and paddling diagonally across stream will help reposition yourself to a bank. Chest waders secured with a wading belt will furnish some buoyancy, and an inflatable vest or coast-guard approved life vest is useful in providing additional floatation. Avoid panicking because you may tumble downstream in a head-over-heels manner exposing yourself to potential injury. Lie back and swim it out.

Neoprene chest waders provide both buoyancy and a slimmer profile which lessens the amount of exposed surface area and helps to trap air inside the waders. Neoprenes are the safest waders available. Even if you fall and take in some water the waders can warm it up.

During a plunge it's difficult to give up your precious fly rod and reel. Try to hold it upright while swimming or if possible you may choose to toss it bank side. Throw the rod like a spear so it lands butt first; it is less likely to break when thrown in this manner.

Some streams afford troublesome wading. Idaho's Fall River is appropriately named not only for its scenic waterfalls but for its many fallen anglers. It has swift currents with unbelievably odd-shaped lava boulders and well-greased rocks. Nearly every step is a potential trip. Another difficult wading stream is the Madison. When wading such streams use utmost caution.

Hip Boots

Hip boots are good for hiking through wet, brushy areas where you seldom experience a difficult wade; moreover, they are fine for most wetland and beaver pond fishing. The disadvantage is that during a plunge hip boots readily fill with water and severely weigh you down, restricting swimming. Hip boots are a poor choice for difficult and dangerous wading.

Summary

1. Choose well-fitting waders and make sure that the inseam is the correct length so that you can move freely. Too short of an inseam in your waders will disable your leg movements. The use of a wading belt ensures a secure chest fit. A tight fit around the chest traps air in case of an unexpected plunge.

2. Footing. Stream cleats (combination of aluminum cleats and felt) provide the most stable footing on slippery rocks. Felt soles are good on most rocky stream bottoms. Rubber cleats are good on muddy areas.

3. Carry and use a wading staff.

4. Use a life preserver in dangerous wades.

5. At all times have one foot secured. Never move the unsecured foot without the other foot secured.

6. Before wading, take into account the streambed's conditions, depth, and current velocity. Choose the appropriate gear.

Float Tubes and Pontoon Boats

11

Float tubes offer still water anglers tremendous advantages. Their soft nylon/neoprene and water junctions dampen sound production and keep your movements quiet. You still need to pay attention to shadows, but because you sit low in the water your compact silhouette is more difficult for the fish to spot than the silhouette of a standing and moving shoreline angler. Generally speaking, float tubes allow for an effective close approach without alarming the fish.

Float tubes provide access to waters otherwise unreachable like brush-choked or boggy shorelines where fish often cruise for minnows and nymphs, but float tubes can also give you easy and lethal access to offshore areas such as weed beds, submerged springs, ledges, and islands. Because the tube, waders, and fins can weigh less than twelve pounds, a float tube is highly mobile and can be backpacked into remote lakes and ponds. Float tubers can easily access hundreds of places inaccessible to conventional boats that must be trailered or portaged. In addition, many waters closed for motorized craft are open to float tubing. Hence, a float tube is ideal for the still water fly rodder because it offers us a close approach to places we could otherwise never fish. Because float tubes are propelled and steered by fins on your feet, they leave both hands free to fish.

Select a float tube in the medium to high price range. Quality craft feature double or triple stitching of durable nylon with non-corrosive zippers immune to rust. With a quick-draining mesh bottom, the float tube can readily dry off for transport inside your automobile. A stripping apron assists fly rodders with their casting by providing a dry place to hold strips of fly line in tangle-free coils. A double backrest provides a comfortable

back support, additional floatation, and storage for a lunch, drinking water, and perhaps an extra reel. A deep seat adds to the comfort level of a good float tube. In addition, ample side pockets furnish plenty of storage areas for easily accessed gear like extra fly boxes, pliers, insect net, sun block lotion, and the like. Consequently, you can keep a complete assortment of tackle, rain gear, and a camera at your fingertips while fishing. Moreover, a suspender system and backpack straps attached by detachable D-rings make transporting the tube–as well as entering and exiting the water–not only convenient but safe.

Neoprene waders are preferable to conventional waders for many float tube anglers because neoprene insulates you from the cold water temperatures, especially on early spring and late fall mornings and evenings. Neoprene booties worn over stocking foot waders provide extra comfort, protection, and warmth. If neoprene waders spring a leak, the inside water soon warms from the angler's body heat and therefore permits some degree of comfort.

Fins should be heavy duty and, most importantly, properly fitted. Overly tight fins will cut circulation and your feet will quickly become cold. A safety strap on comfortably fitting fins will prevent their loss should one or both of the fins ever become displaced in the water. If lost, floating fins are obviously much easier to find than sinking models, and some fins are even designed to fit over boot foot waders. Force fins are efficient to use, and because they curve upwards, they tolerate some land walking.

For safety's sake float tubes are limited to still water use and not for river usage. In fast currents float tubes are dangerous because your feet can snag on underwater obstructions making the craft treacherous to control.

A secondary floatation chamber is insurance against a leaking tube. A coast guard approved life preserver should be either worn or stored for ready access. A flashlight is a must for dawn, dusk and night time float tubing.

Float tubes are available in doughnut shapes, open fronted U boat designs, and pontoon craft models. The doughnut style is the least expensive float tube; in addition, their high backs and side pockets keep out splashing waves.

Useful accessories include a mesh creel, Velcro rod holders, anchor systems, insulated drink holders and video depth sonar (a "fish finder").

Avoid either over-inflating or under-inflating the tube. Optimal air pressure is 3-4 lbs; use a float tube gauge to check your air pressure. Inflate the tube until the wrinkles on the covering are just evened out. Under-inflation causes the float tube to ride so low in the water that it is burdensome to propel. Because sun exposure increases the air pressure, over-inflation may split the float tube's cover.

Open-ended (U-boat) designs allow for easier entries and exits on the water, and consequently they are safest in emergencies because they permit speedier exits. In addition, U-boat designs are easier to propel than the dough-nut-shaped float tubes, which means they are faster on the water, and finally, their general open-end design offers more comfort to the fly rodder than the doughnut-shaped float tubes because the U-boats free your legs to kick and move whereas the doughnut shape somewhat constricts leg movement. In addition, U-boat bladders weigh less than the rubber truck inner tubes used in doughnut float tubes, which means they can be inflated by mouth, an advantage that negates the necessity for an air pump, which is both heavy and cumbersome to pack. Consequently, U-boat float tubes are ideal for backpacking use because air pumps are both heavy and cumbersome to pack. One slight disadvantage is that their open fronts don't allow you to lean on them to steady your elbows.

Pontoon boats are propelled by either fins or oars. They allow you to sit up higher in the water and rest your feet. The higher sitting position allows for easier casting. In fact, because pontoon boats come equipped with seats and rests, they are the most comfortable personal watercraft. Perhaps best of all, pontoon boats can be used on both streams and lakes: big rivers, small rivers, some big creeks, and almost all lakes and ponds. Some models of pontoon boats can safely navigate class III rapids. Streams can be fished with both hands free because the boat can be controlled by the fins. Easy exit and entry is another advantage.

A float tube's inherent safety features are that they catch less wind than a boat. Also, the low profile and large keel (legs) make them stable by being difficult to capsize. Air leaks usually tend to be slow and permit anglers sufficient time to reach shore. Nevertheless, you should carefully inspect and examine the tube twice a year for cracks and sunlight deterioration.

Needless to say, perhaps, it is dangerous to flip over in a float tube, and although this rarely happens, if it does a fast exit is the best medicine. Regardless of the design you choose, make sure it comes with a

quick release buckle.

Lightning strikes are one of my primary fears on the water because a sudden thunderstorm can find you far from shore. Since you are the highest profile around and you are holding a lightning rod (graphite) in your hand, your danger is real. Anticipate storms by quickly getting off the water before the storm can reach your position.

Here again, as in all fly fishing situations, use common sense. In some regions of the country alligators and cottonmouth snakes may pose a threat to anglers. On salt water, a shark may even be attracted to the seal-like movements of an angler in a float tube. Exercise caution with float tubes and pontoon boats wherever you are.

12

DRIFT BOATS

DRIFT BOAT FLY FISHING

It was the kind of day I love to fish. I pulled with long oar strokes to cross the river's heavy flow as the boat glided swiftly through the standing waves of the run. My goal was the shallows on the opposite bank. Here on this roadless expanse of the Henry's Fork of the Snake River, the lush riparian growth makes that shoreline impenetrable to the wading angler.

My three sons—Jason (11), Brett (10), and Jordan (9)—were armed with some of my favorite old fly rods, and our pet Doberman, Babe, was standing guard in the bow. As we approached the far bank and I continued to slow the boat's descent, all three boys started casting their elk hair caddisflies toward rising fish. A trout quickly rose and inhaled the first offering; soon, the second fly had a trout, too. In his excitement, Jordan recast over the two struggling fish and now we had three tangled lines. Babe got into the melee by dominating the bow's casting deck, barking loudly at the struggling fish as they leaped and fought wildly. I dropped the anchor to help with the excitement. The trout were tangled up with each other; finally I managed to release the 15 and 16 inch rainbows back into the Fork. Then, I untangled the lines. No sooner had I pulled anchor and returned to the oars than my young fly fishermen attempted to beat each other's casts to the next good-looking lie. Soon, another trout was hooked and the tangles returned. It was a slapdash day filled with fired-up kids, dog, and trout. But it was also a perfect June day to drift

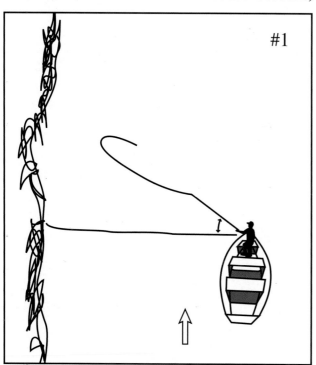

#1

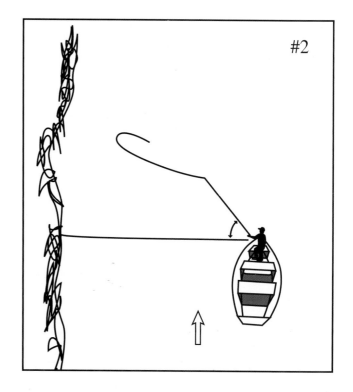

#2

fish the Henry's Fork.

Drift boat fishing is a splendid way to teach inexperienced fly fishermen the significance of a drag-free presentation; likewise, drift boat fishing is an almost ideal method for fishing dry flies. The bank-side fish are usually within comfortable casting distances of about 30 feet, and a drag-free float is simple to achieve if the boat is oared to match the pace of the fly. The rising trout generate excitement. Fishing with three inspired boys in the same boat, however, calls for some sort of rules.

Effective drift boat rules are as follows: (1) across-stream presentation, (2) quartering across-stream presentation, and (3) parallel casting presentation. In addition, some helpful drift boat fishing techniques will be discussed. These principles are intended to improve your success at float fishing.

The across-stream and quartering across-stream presentations clear the way for prolonged drag-free drifts with fewer entanglements. The choice of which presentation to select depends upon the speed of the drifting boat relative to the drifting fly. When the boat is moving faster than the fly, make a quartering downstream cast. This cast is made at an acute angle as measured from directly across stream. The greater the difference between boat speed and fly speed, the greater the acute angle. (See Diagrams 1&2)

On the other hand, when the boat moves slower than the fly, use the across-stream cast. This cast is made straight across the stream at a right angle. (See Diagram 3)

If the boat moves considerably slower than the fly, then the cast may need to be made quartering upstream. (See Diagram 4) All of these quartering and across-stream presentations can extend and prolong a fly's

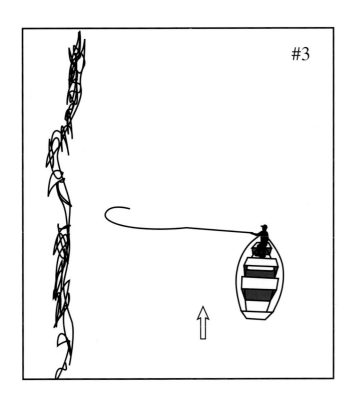

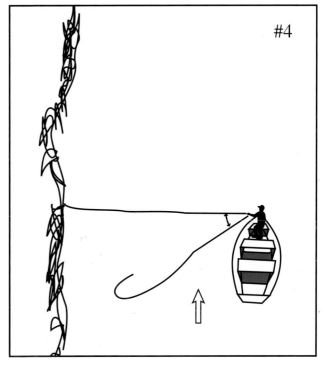

drift by compromising the cast's position in relationship to the different boat and fly current speeds.

To prevent distress when two or more fly fishermen are casting from the same boat, parallel casting is essential. For instance, the bow and the stern anglers should cast parallel to each other. (See Diagram 5) Otherwise, dissimilar casts made at the same time will likely intersect and tangle. If the casters choose not to cast parallel, then they must alternate casting by taking turns. Of course, when the action is fast, this taking turns suffers. In general, I don't recommend fishing three people from

a boat but at times it's very difficult to leave home a friend or one of your children.

If the fly fishers follow these simple casting guidelines, the oarsman can now greatly influence the fly's potency. The oarsman must constantly observe the line and the fly's drift, positioning the boat for accurate casting into the targeted feeding lanes. The oarsman adjusts the boat's speed by rowing upstream or downstream in an attempt to prolong the fly's presentation. The fly lines can be mended by changing the boat's speed and position. An experienced oarsman can ease the fisherman's job by improving and prolonging the fly's presentation.

A drift boat can quickly and advantageously put you into otherwise inaccessible fish lies. A disadvantage to fishing in a drift boat is that it may only give you one cast at the area. This disadvantage is somewhat overcome by allowing you to fish a lot more water. Also, you fish to the most aggressive takers; those that

#5

#6

immediately strike on the first cast.

The backcast is made relatively high. A high backcast helps protect the others in the boat from a roving fly. To accomplish a high backcast make certain your forward line is straightened out before you backcast; next, aim the backcast higher than you would normally do when bank fishing. When the backcast is angled higher you must counter balance the forward cast by driving it at a lower angle. (See Diagram 6)

This casting technique is also effective in windy conditions because the angled delivery places the cast line lower to the water where the streamside vegetation has buffered the wind.

Line mending lengthens your fly's presentation. Use common sense in deciding which direction to mend; for instance, when the boat is moving more slowly than the fly, mend in an upstream direction. Conversely; when the boat is moving faster than the fly, mend downstream. If you mend in the wrong direction the error is instantly apparent because the fly will drag badly. The mend's purpose is to prolong a drag-free presentation, and a drag-free presentation dramatically boosts your

chances for success.

In drift boating, casting is used to position the fly and to dry it, while line mending and boat maneuvers direct the presentation of the fly.

The cast's length and the boat's distance are adjusted according to the wariness of the fish and the prevailing water conditions. Clear water and alert fish call for longer casts and greater boat distances; stained water and naïve fish, however, call for shorter casting and boat distances.

Fish holding just under the surface are less watchful and more vulnerable to a fly because their vision is restricted. Fish holding in deeper water have a larger field of vision; likewise, fish holding in deep water can more readily spot the boat. As a result, deep holding fish are more troublesome to approach than shallow holding fish.

Silence is vital for a close approach; furthermore, banging a boat bottom drives the fish away. I experienced the effect of boat noise one year when I helped with the netting of Fall Chinook Salmon on Oregon's Chetco River. The biologists would bang the bottom of their aluminum jet sled whenever they wanted to herd the fish into the awaiting net.

It's always a good idea to carpet aluminum boat floors with a throw rug and line the tackle trays and casting deck with rubber mats. These measures can silence a boat and allow a fly fisher a closer approach.

Be sure to avoid exaggerated casting motions. Fish are constantly on alert for birds of prey, and a false caster waiving

his rod arm can mimic a bird's swooping motion. Limit the false casting to a bare minimum; if necessary, dry the fly on an absorbent cloth rather than by false casting. With a silent and a still approach, the feeding fish may be only a short cast away. A drag-free presentation dramatically boosts your chances for success.

There's simply no doubt about it: accurate casting enhances drift boat fishing. Being able to hit a bank-side target the first time makes a great difference in productivity. Learning to negotiate underneath tree limbs by controlling line loops is also a valuable skill.

To help insure that you hit targets with your first cast, try having the appropriate length of line already stripped from your reel before you cast; this will limit the length of your cast but it will also make your cast more accurate. From trial and error adjust to find the optimal line length outside of the reel. Simply cast this line length, and, if it looks long, pull up some on the forward cast. Practice at becoming proficient at hitting the target the first time.

The ability to quickly read water is vital to successful drift boat fishing. Speed

reading fish lies, of course, is a skill that only comes from experience, but even a rookie can react to an upcoming lie by recasting, repositioning or mending.

To hit each lie in pocket water requires frequent casting. Because holding lies in pocket water pass quickly, inexperienced anglers tend to panic. Instead, be patient and choose the best lies. Not even the most experienced angler can cast to every fish. In float fishing, the ability to instantly read water is a great advantage; consequently, the more miles you drift, the better you will become at reading lies and the better you will also become at communicating.

Good communication between the oarsman and the caster is essential because the oarsman is usually the first to locate the new lies. By verbally describing the

characteristics and location of downstream holding water as the boat drifts, the oarsman can assist the caster by mentally preparing the caster ahead of time to make the appropriate cast. Develop a system of communication that describes distances and clockwise locations as a basis for immediate mutual understanding. The longer you talk together the better and the quicker you will be able to understand each other. Drift boat fly fishers often use a kind of verbal shorthand to increase their success rate. For example, to alert the caster to an upcoming lie, the oarsman might use the position of the hour hand and approximate distance by calling out, "2 o'clock pocket at 30 feet" or "10 o'clock current seam at 40 feet" or something similar.

In short, drift boat fishing is a great way

to experience a river system. We can learn of new prime lies to return to when wading or bank fishing. Drift boating reveals where and what insects are hatching on the river at a particular time. No doubt about it: it's just plain exciting to cover lots of water and catch its most aggressive fish.

KNOTS 13

The basic steps in tying any knot correctly are: (1) forming, (2) lubricating, (3) drawing tightly, and (4) trimming.

Forming the knot is vital. It must be correctly tied; otherwise, the knot will not tighten properly and fail. Form each knot slowly and carefully.

A lubricated knot is most easily tightened. Use saliva or water to moisten the area to be drawn together. This reduces both friction and heat which can weaken the line.

Carefully tighten the knot slowly to avoid any overlapping loops. These overlaps can weaken the connection.

Finally trim the tag end close to the knot. This tag end serves no useful purpose other than providing a place to draw up the knot.

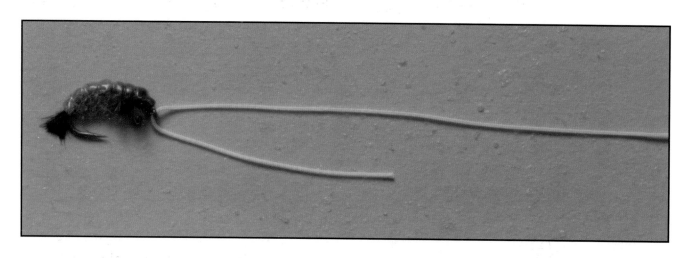

CLINCH KNOT: Provides a fast attachment of tippet to fly.

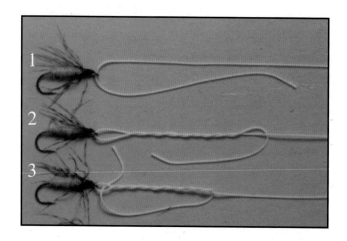

1. Pass leader through hook eye with about 6 inches of the tag end.
2. Hold fly securely in one hand and wrap the tag end 5 times around the standing leader.
3. Pass tag end back through the loop near the hook eye.
4. Lubricate, draw tightly, avoid any overlapping loops, and trim tag end

IMPROVED CLINCH KNOT: Provides a strong attachment of tippet to fly.

Complete the first 3 steps of the clinch knot. Then proceed as follows:

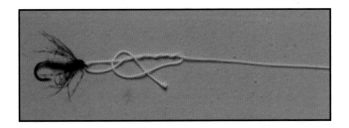

Pass the tag end through the large loop. Lubricate, draw tightly, avoid any overlapping loops, and trim the tag end.

B.C. KNOT: Provides the strongest connection of tippet to fly.

1. Pass a doubled section of leader through the hook eye with about 6 inches of tag end.
2. Hold fly securely in one hand and wrap the tag end 5 times around the standing leader.
3. Pass the tag end back through the small loop near the hook eye. Lubricate,   draw tightly, avoid

overlapping loops, and trim tag end. (Note this is the same knot as the clinch knot but it is tied with a doubled loop.)

DUNCAN LOOP: The Duncan Loop is used to join the tippet to the fly. It provides an excellent sliding loop that can be tightened anywhere on the standing part of the leader. The loop size can be easily adjusted. I like it for heavy tippets because the loop does not impair the action of the fly. A stiff leader traditionally knotted to the fly would be too stiff of a junction and impair the fly's action.

1. Put the leader tag through the hook eye with about 8 inches of tag end remaining. Keep tag leader parallel to the standing leader.
2. Turn the tag end so it comes back underneath the 2 parallel strands. Wind the tag end around these 2 parallel strands. Make 5 wraps around the parallel strands (inside the loop).
3. Lubricate, draw tightly by pulling both tag and standing tag end.

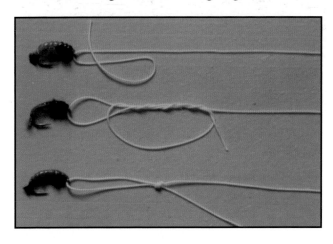

SURGEON'S LOOP:
This knot makes a fast loop. It is useful for loop-to-loop connections.

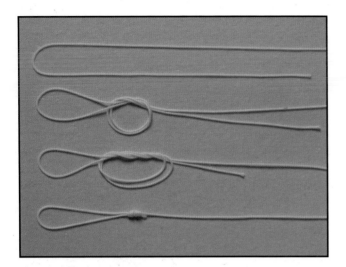

1. Make a loop and bring tag end back.
2. Make at least 2 or up to 5 overhand knots with the doubled leader.
3. Lubricate, draw tightly, avoid overlapping loops, and trim tag end.

PERFECTION LOOP:
This makes a strong, dependable loop for loop-to-loop connections.

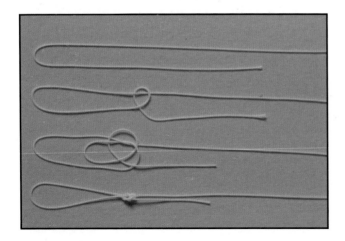

1. Make a loop.
2. Make 2 loops from the tag end. Pull the front loop through the first loop.

3. Lubricate, draw tight, and trim tag end.

BLOOD or BARREL KNOT:
This knot joins 2 leaders of equal or unequal diameters. The knot works best with leaders under 20# test. Heavier leaders can be too stiff to easily tie this knot.

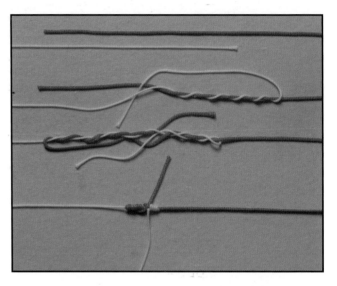

1. Bring the tag ends together in opposite directions.
2. Make an X with tag ends and make 4 to 5 turns around the standing portions of the leaders with the tag ends. Pass the tag ends through the center in opposite directions.
3. Lubricate, draw tightly, avoid any overlapping loops, and trim tag ends.

SURGEON'S KNOT:

This knot quickly joins 2 leaders of equal or unequal diameters. It can also provide a dropper if one of its tags ends is left untrimmed. It can be tied as a double or as a triple by tying 2 or 3 overhand knots. The triple knot is the stronger one of the two.

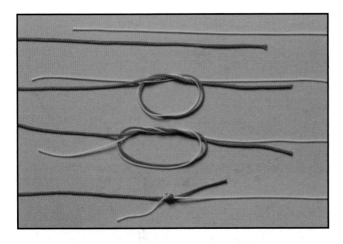

1. Assemble the 2 leaders to be joined (tag end opposite).

2. Make 2 (for the Double Surgeon's Knot) or 3 (for the Triple Surgeon's Knot) overhand knots. All are tied in the same direction (like a Granny Knot).

3. Lubricate, draw ends tightly, avoid overlapping loops, and trim the tag ends.

ALBRIGHT KNOT:

Excellent knot for connecting lines of unequal diameters.

Commonly used to join the fly line to the backing. It is useful to connect the leader to the fly line (it makes a stronger connection than the nail knot).

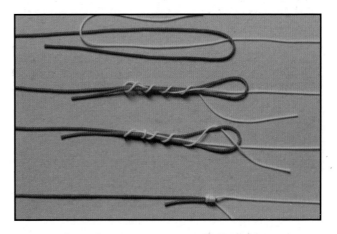

1. Make a loop in the end of the fly line. Pass the backing or the leader through this loop.

2. Make at least 5 twists. You can make up to 10 twists if you want a longer knot that will slide through the rod's line guides more easily. Pass the tag end through the fly line loop in the opposite direction.

3. Lubricate, draw tightly, avoid any overlapping loops, and trim the tag end.

NAIL or TUBE KNOT:

This one provides a smooth connection of fly line to the leader butt.

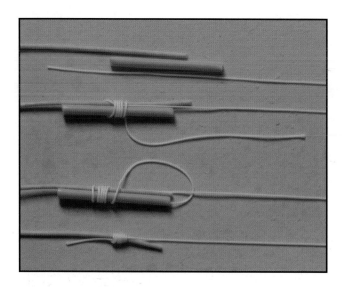

1.   Assemble fly line, nail or tube, and leader.
2.   Wrap leader tag end around fly line, tube (nail), and standing leader. Make at least 5 wraps. Pull leader tag end through tube or pass in close proximity to nail. Next, pull tube or nail out.
3.   Draw knot tightly without any overlapping. Trim tag ends.

ANGLER ETIQUETTE

Recently the Salt Lake Tribune reported a headline story entitled "Angler Etiquette on the Decline" and "River-rage incident is part of a disturbing trend in a peaceful sport." On November 13, 2004, one man pulled a handgun to end a heated confrontation. An angler was fishing from a mid-stream rock in Utah's Green River when a drift boat closely crossed over his fishing hole. Jumping from the rock, the man grabbed the drift boat. An argument ensued that ended when the boat angler drew his gun.

Our streams are not Los Angeles freeways. For many, fly fishing is a way to escape the cities' crowds. For years fly fishing has been a peaceful sport. But lately the many anglers seeking solitude have taken out their frustration by being combative fishermen.

Fishing etiquette is becoming a thing of the past. Rude behavior is on the increase. Recently I had my prized fly rod outfit shoplifted while I was sitting on my tailgate

taking off my waders. I had carefully set it down alongside my vest and while I was busy changing someone stole it. My name was clearly engraved on my rod.

We must put a stop to this rude behavior trend. One of the reasons that I have enjoyed fly fishing for so many years is that my fellow anglers have been so respectful of others. I have made many friends while fishing a stream. Fly fishermen have been the elite sportsmen. They care for the environment by practicing conservation and they have been helpful and courteous to others.

I have met some rude anglers. One incident occurred along a desert river. My friend and I started to descend a steep rocky trail when we encountered a mass rattlesnake migration. The snakes were everywhere and frightened, we returned back to the truck. I have never witnessed

so many aggressive snakes. As we were preparing to leave, a grumpy angler parked by us and started ragging on us for fishing his favorite spot. He was so rude that we failed to warn him about the rattlers. He started hiking down the trail wearing only shorts and tennis shoes. My friend and I looked at each other smiling. In a few moments the enraged angler returned, upset over our failure to warn him. We left before a brawl could break out. We should have warned him even though he started the ruckus.

Let us return to the days when the fly fisherman was the elite sportsman. Always be respectful of others. Ask before fishing or getting close to another angler. Be friendly and inquire about his success. He may be a helpful source of current information. I'm a prolific fly tier and I commonly give my successful flies away. When I later see the angler he is now a friend and a valuable source of information. Making friends with other anglers is rewarding because I have learned of many new, good places and productive methods.

Let us all be on our best behavior at all times. Do not disturb another angler's fishing spot. Let him know that you are heading away from where he is fishing. Don't wade, walk, or boat near his water. Skirt it widely and quietly. Simply follow the "Golden Rule." It works.

Fly fishermen on the average are highly successful people. Their education level and income are in the top percentiles. Correspondingly our behavior on a stream should match these demographics. Walking too close to a stream bank can alarm the fish and should be avoided. Your silhouette and tramping can cause both alarming sights and vibrations. Find a way to give another angler's water a wide berth. He will respect you for your actions.

Wading and boating require a detour so that you avoid the area being fished. Pass your boat quietly, well away from their spot. Don't splash the oars and don't make waves.

If your water is too crowded, be flexible in your plans by trying another place. Perhaps you may find a more productive location.

Practice strict catch and release. Limit your take to only what you will really use. Obey the laws for they were designed to preserve our fisheries. Biologists' research data went into their enactments.

Catch and release is simple. First, play the fish in as quickly as possible. I use heavier tippets than most and either small-barbed or non-barbed hooks. Turn the fish upside down because this disorients the fish and reduces struggling. Grab the fly with either forceps or firmly with your fingers. Back the hook out the way it went in. If the barb is being stubborn, press the hook in a little then pull the barb away from

the snagged tissue and pull the hook free. Forceps should be clamped closely to the barbed area. Pull on the fly in a straight path. Return the fish back into the water as soon as possible or better yet remove the hook while the fish is still submerged. Hold the fish upright with its head upstream then give it time to catch its breath. You can aid in its respiration by moving the fish back and forth pumping water through its gills. When revived, the fish readily swims back to deeper water.

A soft landing net is helpful in controlling a fish. Wet hands tend to remove less of a fish's protective slime coating. This coating is a barrier against viral and bacterial infections so a fish should be handled minimally.

Fish are released so that we can catch them again. Fly fishing is a "Green Sport" that treads lightly on the environment.

Finally, become actively involved in political positions affecting our water's environment. Study the issues and vote according to what you think is right. Let's preserve our sport, for it is truly a lifetime one.

Bibliography

Arnold, Bob. *Steelhead & the Floating Line*. Portland, Oregon: Frank Amato Publications, Inc. 1993.

Arnold, Bob. *Steelhead Water*. Portland, Oregon: Frank Amato Publications, Inc. 1993.

Combs, Trey. *Steelhead Fly Fishing*. New York, N.Y.: The Lyons Press. 1991.

Cordes, Ron, and Kaufmann, Randall. *Lake Fishing With A Fly*. Portland, Oregon: Frank Amato Publications, Inc. 1984.

Kreh, Lefty. *Fly Fishing in Saltwater*. Third Edition. New York, N.Y.: The Lyons Press. 1997.

McNally, Bob. *Fishermen's Knots, Fishing Rigs, And How To Use Them*. Jacksonville, FL: McNally Outdoor Productions. 1993.

Schollmeyer, Jim. *Hatch Guide for Western Streams*. Portland, Oregon: Frank Amato Publications, Inc. 1997.

Scott, Jock. *Greased Line Fishing for Salmon [and Steelhead]*. Portland, Oregon: Frank Amato Publications, Inc. 1982.

Sheway, John, and Maxwell, Forest. *Fly Fishing For Summer Steelhead*. Portland, Oregon: Frank Amato Publications, Inc. 1996.

Sheway, John. *Mastering The Spring Creeks: A Fly Angler's Guide*. Portland, Oregon: Frank Amato Publications, Inc. 1994.

Whitlock, Dave. *Dave Whitlock's Guide To Aquatic Trout Foods*. Guilford, Connecticut: The Globe Pequot Press. 1976.

Glossary

Anadromous A fish that's reared in fresh water, migrates to salt water to mature, and returns to freshwater to spawn.

Annelid An aquatic worm.

Antron A synthetic yarn that sparkles light. Used in fly tying to simulate air bubbles.

Attractor Fly A pattern designed to excite a strike.

Backcast The part of the fly cast that reaches behind the caster.

Backing A line used to take up space between the fly reel's arbor and the fly line; most commonly used is Dacron or polypropylene line. Acts as additional line when a fish runs out of all the line.

Baetis A mayfly species that's an important aquatic food source. The blue wing olive (bwo) is a common example.

Barrel Knot A knot used to join two leader sections of similar diameters. Also called a blood knot.

Bead Head Fly A metal or plastic bead that simulates a thorax on a nymph or wet fly. Also this bead adds additional weight to the fly.

Blood Knot Same as a barrel knot.

Buck Tail The hair of a whitetail deer's tail used in constructing fly wings. Most commonly used in tying streamers.

Buoyancy The tendency for an object to rise or float to the surface.

Caddis Common aquatic insect resembling a moth when in flight. At rest its wings fold in a pup tent fashion. An important source of fish nutrition.

Cast Using a rod to throw the line.

Casting Arc The rod's path during a complete cast.

CDC "Cull de Canard" feathers found on the butt area of a duck. They are waterproof because they surround the oil gland of a duck. Useful in tying flies that float.

Chironomid Members of the Diptera family of aquatic insects. Common name is the midge.

Clinch Knot A common knot used for attaching the leader to a hook.

Damselfly An important aquatic insect found in stillwaters. Resembles a dragonfly but is much thinner and somewhat more graceful.

Dead Drift The fly drifts at the same rate as the current, almost as if it was not attached to the leader.

Deer Hair A hollow body hair from a deer. Used to tie floating flies or buoyant set flies.

Double Taper Fly Line Both fly line ends are equally tapered. The middle of the line is a thick level line. Excellent line for casting smooth loops.

Drag (a) An unnatural motion of the fly caused by the line and leader pulling against the current. (b) Resistance applied to a fly reel's spool designed to tire a fish's fighting

Drag Free Same as Dead Drift.

Dragonfly An aquatic insect common in stillwaters. The adult flies like a helicopter. Usually bright fluorescent colors and large in size.

Dropper A second fly tied on a leader tippet.

Dry Fly A fly fished on top of the water's surface.

Dry Fly Floatant A waterproof chemical applied to the fly to prevent it from being wetted. Aids in the fly floating on the surface film.

Dubbing The body material used on a fly. Usually ties from natural fur or synthetic materials twisted onto a waxed thread.

Dun Adult aquatic inset that has emerged from the water.

Eddy A section of a stream that is less disturbed than the surrounding water. Sometimes moves in a slow whirlpool motion.

Elk Hair Hollow body hair from an elk. Useful in tying floating flies.

Emerger The life phase of an aquatic insect that emerges from the water's bottom to its surface to change into an adult life stage. Readily available to fish predation.

Epilimnion The layer of water above the thermocline.

False Cast The part of a fly cast used to lengthen and to direct the fly line. The line is kept moving forward and backward without settling down to the water or the ground.

Fluorocarbon A leader or tippet material which is a polyvinglidenfluoride. It has the same refraction index as water making it seem to disappear when submerged. It also is not affected by sunlight's deterioration.

Fly Casting The method used to present the fly to the desired target.

Fly Line Line made of tapered plastic coating over a braided dacron core. Multiple designs made for floating, sinking and casting.

Fly Reel The fishing reel used to store the fly line.

Fly Rod A fishing rod designed to cast a fly line.

Forward Cast That portion of the fly cast that occurs in front of the caster. Used to either false cast or to deliver the fly to the target.

Freestone Stream A stream type where the majority of water comes from tributaries. Its source is usually snow melt or rainfall. Usually found in canyons with steeper gradients resulting in faster current flows. Subject to unstable flows with periods of run-off and drought.

Graphite Fly Rod Most common fly rod material used to date. It is both strong and light weight. Accurate flexing ratios are obtainable.

Hackle A feather with non-adhering barbs. Commonly found on the necks of chickens.

Hackles The neck feathers of a chicken. Stiff hackles come from the males while soft hackles are found on the females.

Hatch Flies that have recently emerged and are available for fish predation.

Hen Hackle Soft hackle found on female or hen chickens.

Herl Long barbule feathers found on peacock or ostrich birds. Useful in tying the bodies of flies.

Hypolimnion The layer of water below the thermocline.

Indicator A floating material placed on a fly leader used to visually indicate a fish's strike. Used in fishing nymphs and small dry flies.

Intermediate Fly Line The slowest sink rate fly line. This line is useful in presenting flies just under the surface and suspending the fly over the submerged weed beds.

Knotless Tapered Leader A tapered leader made from a single piece of leader without knots. You can't make these yourself. They must be purchased from a store.

Knotted Tapered Leader A tapered leader made by knotting various diameters and lengths of leaders together. The surgeon's knot or blood (barrel) knot are used to join the sections. You can make these yourself and custom design them.

Larva Immature aquatic insects that are usually bottom dwellers. Nymphs are used to imitate them.

Leader A portion of monofilament between the fly line and the fly. Usually tapered so it can be cast with accuracy and delicacy.

Level Fly Line A level untapered line usually used as a shooting line.

Littoral Zone A shallow water section of a lake where sunlight can penetrate and cause submerged plant growth.

Loop Connection The joining of the flyline to the leader or the shooting head to the running line with interlocking loops. Loops are easy to change and pass through the line guides with ease.

Mayfly An important aquatic insect used as a common food source for fish. A complete life cycle with four stages: pupa, larva, dun and spinner. Found in both streams and in still waters.

Mending Line A procedure used to change the position of the line and leader while it is on or in the water. Its used to achieve a drag-free presentation. It can be used to either slow down or to speed up the drift of the fly.

Midge Small Dipterans that are also called chironomids. Important source of fish food. Commonly called Gnats.

Monofilament A clear leader made of nylon or fluorocarbon. It provides an invisible connection between fly line and fly.

Nail Knot A knot used to join the fly line to the leader.

Narrow Tight Loop A term describing how the fly line travels as it is cast through the air. It can be described as "U" shaped with the paralled sides of the U close together. It is an efficient casting method providing fast line speeds.

Nymph Immature life stages of aquatic insects. Important fish staple.

Open Wide Loop This is opposite of a narrow tight loop. As the line passes through the air the "U" shape is open in that the parallel sides are far apart. Inefficient casting method causing slow line speeds, although it provides a delicate delivery.

Pelagic Zone The surface portion of a deep body of water.

Presentation The method of delivering the fly to the fish in a natural way.

Pupa The transitional life stage between the larva and the adult insect.

Retrieve The pulling of the fly line to simulate a natural food's motion.

Riffle A fast current section of a stream that flows over a rocky bottom.

Riparian Plants and objects next to a river bank.

Rise A fish taking a fly usually at the surface.

Roll-cast A casting method that eliminates the backcast. Useful when casting in areas where brush occurs at your back.

Run A fast flowing section of a stream.

"S" Cast A cast which deliberately places slack line into the delivery. This slack line lays in "S" curves on the water allowing a drag free float.

Scour Erosion caused by running water.

Scud Fresh water shrimp which is an aquatic food source.

Setting (striking) the Hook The motion of pulling the hook into the fish's mouth.

Shooting Head A short tapered fly line designed for making long casts with ease. They come in a wide range of sinking rates. They are easily changed with loop connections.

Snake Guides A looped wire line guide.

Spinner A mayfly's egg-laying life stage.

Stonefly A family of aquatic insects commonly found in freestone streams.

Streamer A fly designed to resemble a baitfish.

Stripping Guide Large metal or ceramic guide found close to the fly rod's real seat. Designed to collect the line efficiently as it is cast or retrieved.

Surface Film The top of the water which is similar to an elastic membrane created by the surface tension.

Surface Tension The liquid's surface behaves like a membrane. It's caused by molecular attraction between the water molecules. The property of a liquid that allows heavier-than-water items to float.

Surgeon's Knot Excellent knot to join two leaders together that are similar or different diameters.

Terrestrial A land-based insect which is commonly eaten by fish.

Thermocline A layer of water in a lake where the temperature gradient is cooler than the water above and warmer than the water below. A zone where the temperature gradient is the greatest. (Widest range)

Tippet The portion of the leader that joins the fly to the tapered leader.

Vest A vest with multiple pockets designed to carry fly fishing tools and tackle.

Waders High topped waterproof pants used to wade.

Weight Forward Line A tapered fly line with its tapered section in the front end of the line. Designed to shoot line with ease. Its shooting line or rear taper is a small diameter level line.

Wet Fly Any fly fished below the surface.

Wet Fly Swing A presentation where the fly swings in an arc across the current.

Wind Knot An overhand knot caused by casting. It greatly reduces the leader's strength.

X The leader diameter designation. The actual leader diameter can be determined in thousandths of an inch by subtraction. The X designation from the number 11. For example: a 4X leader (11-4=7) is .007".

Index